Felicitas Bachmann

PLAYMOBIL
The Story of a Smile

HEEL

For Carla, Finn, and the millions of other Playmobil fans, large and small—and for Hans Beck, without whom the world of toys would be a significant 2.9 inches poorer.

Imprint

HEEL Verlag GmbH
Gut Pottscheidt
53639 Königswinter, Germany
Tel.: +49 (0) 22 23 92 30-0
Fax: +49 (0) 22 23 92 30-13
info@heel-verlag.de
www.heel-verlag.de

© 2006 HEEL Verlag GmbH, Königswinter, Germany

® PLAYMOBIL
pronounced: "plāy–mō–bēēl"
geobra Brandstätter GmbH & Co. KG, Zirndorf/Germany
www.playmobil.com

licensed by: BAVARIA SONOR, Bavariafilmplatz 8,
82301 Geiselgasteig, Germany

All rights, including for reprints, duplication in any form and translation into other languages, are reserved by the publisher. It is forbidden to photocopy or to save, systematically exploit or distribute this book or any parts thereof by means of any electronic or mechanical system without written permission from the publisher.

Author: Felicitas Bachmann, Dortmund, Germany

Cover photo:
© by geobra Brandstätter GmbH & Co. KG

Interior photos:
All © by geobra Brandstätter GmbH & Co. KG except:
© Bachmann: p. 29 bottom, p. 44 bottom right,
p. 46 bottom, p.59 bottom, p. 65 top right, p. 66 bottom,
p. 68, p. 117 centre, p. 130 top left, p. 132 top, p. 137,
p. 167 centre and inside jacket left

© BIG: p. 21
© p. 59: DaimlerChrysler Media Archive
© p. 99: Julia Schnitzer
© p. 134-135: Sven Hanning
© p. 138: Hans Joachim Winkler
© p. 139: Daniela Schabenstiel
© p. 140, 141 top: The Czaika family

© p. 140 bottom: Oliver Schaffer
© p. 142: Oliver Deeg
© p. 144 top: Sven Hanning
© p. 144 bottom: Axel Hennel
© p. 145: Sven Hanning
© p. 150 top right: Herpa
© p. 152-153: Marek Mc Banek
© p. 154 top: Philip Grözinger, bottom: Julia Schnitzer
© p. 155 left: Philip Grözinger, centre: Sebastian Mayer, bottom: C. X. Huth
© p. 156: Men Rabe
© p. 157: Jorge Villalba-Strohecker
© p. 158 top: Ralf Gemein, bottom: Kiki Ahlers
© p. 159 top left: Ralf Gemein, right: Ingo Klöcker
© p. 160-161: Sebastian Meyer
© p. 162: Sven Schmidt
© p. 164 left: from Lesepiraten-Rittergeschichten, p. 9. Author/Illustrator: Martin Klein/Peter Nieländer, © by Loewe Verlag, Bindlach, Germany
© p. 166: Thordis Karlotta Rüggeberg
© p. 167 top centre and right: Andreas Männer, bottom: Andy Jones

English text:
Mary Dobrian, Cologne, Germany

Copy editor:
Ashley Benning, Austin, USA

Typesetting and layout:
Grafikbüro Schumacher, Königswinter, Germany

Lithography:
Petra Hammermann, Collibri, Königswinter, Germany

Printing and production:
Ellwanger Bayreuth, Germany

– All rights reserved –

Printed in Germany

ISBN 3-89880-623-5

Felicitas Bachmann

playmobil
The Story of a Smile

HEEL

Contents

6 Foreword

8 A German success story

34 Dot, dot, dash—and the PLAYMOBIL face was done, or how a little pencil drawing became a peaceful world power

48 From the development desk to the toy counter—three years of work

72 PLAYMOBIL—a timeline

106 A lion in the jail, or what would today's children play with if there were no PLAYMOBIL?

126 Life-sized PLAYMOBIL to get your hands on

134 Caution! PLAYMOBIL can be addictive

146 All around the playroom, or all the places you can put a PLAYMOBIL logo

152 Rembrandt, Tischbein and 10,312 PLAYMOBIL figures—a toy conquers the art world

160 PLAYMOBIL—more than a toy

Foreword

foreword

This is the story of a 2.9-inch tall little man who conquered the world from the small Franconian town of Zirndorf. Within just three decades—along with his 1.7 billion sisters and brothers—he has populated his very own continent: It is blue, its name is PLAYMOBIL Land, and in population, it ranks directly behind Asia.

A long time ago, in February 1972, as the 15 millionth VW Beetle was rolling off the assembly line and becoming the best-selling car in the world, another German success story was quietly and secretly taking shape. Geobra Brandstätter GmbH & Co. KG applied for a patent under the reference number P 22 05 525.0-15.

The object, which would spread throughout the playrooms of the world in the next thirty years like only the Barbie virus or LEGO blocks before it, was described in dry officialese as a "toy figure with body open at the bottom". At first, their inventors simply called them "Klicky"; children all over the world—for whom they were intended—mostly called them by their actual name: PLAYMOBIL.

Thus, Horst Brandstätter—Managing Director, and today the sole owner of the toy manufacturing company—and his then-model maker, Hans Beck, joined the ranks of the great toy inventors. Like Margarethe Steiff with her bears, Ole Kirk Kristiansen with his LEGO blocks and Ruth Handler with the Barbie doll before them, they wrote (toy-making) history.

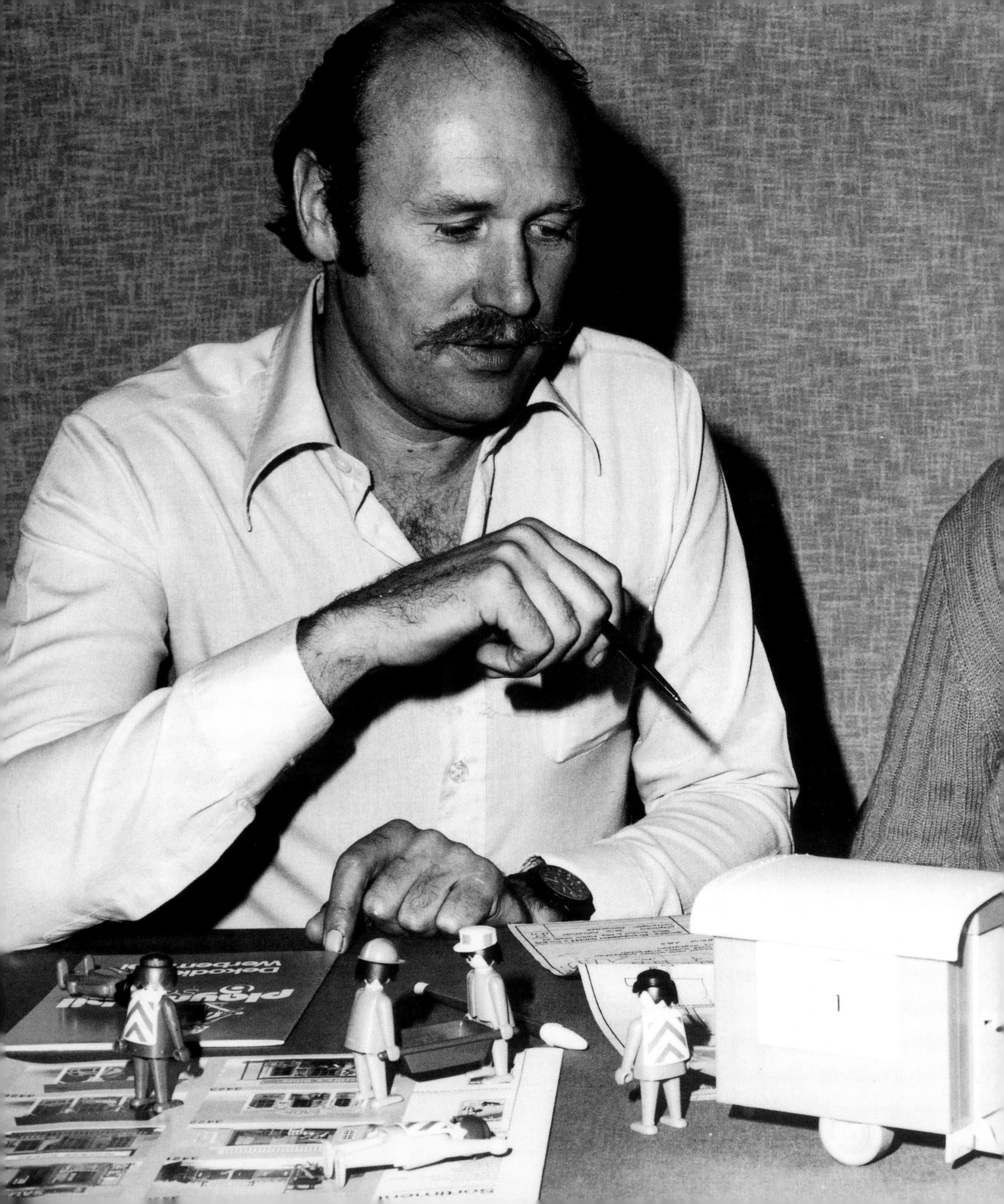

A German success story

PLAYMOBIL—the story sounds as American as a Hollywood fairy tale: from a medium-sized company on the verge of bankruptcy in the early 1970s to Germany's most profitable toy manufacturer. Yet in the beginning, PLAYMOBIL was nothing more than one more product in the long history of the Franconian firm geobra Brandstätter. However, it was a product which would exceed all expectations, which would make geobra famous and successful the world over, and one without which many children's worlds would be less colourful and rich in fantasy. But everything started out very small…

A German success story

In the 1920s and '30s, penny banks and play-grocery items were among the top-selling toys, and cash register penny banks were a worldwide success. They automatically added up coins as they were inserted and opened when a particular sum had been saved.
Up to 1000 penny banks were manufactured daily at geobra and individually tested by inserting coins. Even Horst Brandstätter's grandmother, the senior manager, sat at the assembly table.
For a brief period during the Second World War, the factory was forced to manufacture hand grenades. These would be converted back into penny banks in peacetime.

A German success story

THE BEGINNINGS

In 1876, the trained gunsmith and master locksmith Andreas Brandstätter started his own business in Fürth. With a total of six employees, journeymen and apprentices, the company manufactured fittings and locks for caskets. In 1908, his son Georg took over the firm and renamed it "Metallwarenfabrik Georg Brandstätter".
After moving to the nearby town of Zirndorf, the company was registered as a general commercial partnership in 1926; its business was stated as "the fabrication of metal objects and toys and the commercial trade therewith". The main products were items such as cash registers and scales for toy shops, as well as penny banks and play telephones—a sector to which the company would remain faithful for some time. In the early 1930s, the company name was expanded to include the trademark "geobra" (Georg Brandstätter), and was finally changed to geobra Brandstätter, as it has remained to this day.

Andreas Brandstätter (left), the company's founding father, and his son Georg, who gave the firm its name: geo(rg)bra(ndstätter).

Along with the manufacture of toys began the export of products from Zirndorf to neighbouring countries. Penny banks were a particular hit in England. Catalogues were also printed in several languages.

In the late 1950s, the beloved old wooden rocking-horse was replaced by a plastic horse on wheels. This was made possible by a new blowing technology that allowed for the production of large items that were lightweight and used less material.

A German success story

A NEW GENERATION

In 1952, 19-year-old Horst Brandstätter, a trained mould maker and great-grandson of the company's founder, Andreas, brought a breath of fresh air into the firm. Upon coming of age two years later, he became a partner and won his uncles over to a new material, plastic. He also reorganised the company's production and product range and sought out new sales markets.

The year 1958 marked the dawn of a new era in two different ways: Horst Brandstätter hired Hans Beck as his first model maker, and the Americans invented the hula hoop. Thanks to his good contacts in the USA, Brandstätter heard of the new trend early on and began working meticulously to develop an appropriate production machine. According to company legend, he puzzled day and night over a method which would shape the soft, hot plastic tubes into a round hoop. His breakthrough came within two weeks—and he emerged at the head of the European pack in manufacturing the new hip-spinner.

In the late 1950s, the hula hoop was spinning around millions of German waists. The beloved plastic tube was even immortalised in a film starring Conny Froboess.

German Chancellor Ludwig Erhard inspects a geobra plastic tractor, which, unfortunately, can only carry 220 lbs. Nevertheless, his interest underscores the economic importance of the German toy industry.

TRACTORS AND PIGGIES

Hula hoops began rapidly spinning around everyone's hips, representing the liberated spirit of the dawning "German Economic Miracle". Germany even devoted a film to the phenomenon: In 1959, Cornelia Froboess spun through the cinemas with Hula Hoop Conny, and money was finally flowing into the coffers at geobra—if only for a brief time, since the hula hoop craze was short-lived. Nevertheless, the newly developed machine encouraged the resourceful company chief to envision other toy-manufacturing possibilities as well. Up until that time, so-called blowing technology had only been used for making bottles. The method is simple: A machine-heated plastic tube is inflated by means of air pressure and pressed against the walls of a mould. Why be limited to bottles, thought Brandstätter: He recognised that it was also possible to inflate asymmetrical shapes. The result was the first seamless racing car, followed by small boats and tractors. Horst Brandstätter saw one of the latter on Beck's desk and commented, "We could even make a really big one that you can sit on." No sooner said than done: Beck designed the first steerable riding tractor for children, modelled after the actual Porsche tractor. Later on, an electri-

A German success story

The top sellers being assembled at the branch factory in Markt Erlbach. Riding tractors and cash registers for play groceries were the company's mainstays in the early 1960s.

fied version was developed, with lights, horn and engine noise, but—probably due to its "annoying" sound—it was not such a big success.

In keeping with the rural theme, the company next turned to pigs—to piggy banks, that is. Here, production was already fully automated and even continued over the weekend. "When we opened the gates of the machine shop on Monday morning, thousands of piggy banks came gushing out at us," Horst Brandstätter remembers.

A German success story

Horst Brandstätter's inventive spirit knew no boundaries. Even water-skis and motorboats were part of his product line for a time—and he was not above testing them himself.

Toy grocery shop products could be produced even more cheaply elsewhere. But rather than turning to the Far East, Horst Brandstätter opened a small factory on Malta in 1971. Today, with 750 workers, it is one of the island's most important employers.

OIL TANKS AND WATER-SKIS

However, the competition in the toy industry had its eyes wide open and picked up on every new idea. The price wars became too fierce. In 1964, the company began manufacturing plastic motorboats parallel to the production of toys; oil tanks followed shortly after. In the electronic arena, they experimented with record-players and intercoms. The wealth of ideas knew no bounds. Brandstätter changed saddles again and began working with structure-foam moulding—a completely new method at that time—which functioned like yeast or baking powder in plastic. New machines were needed, costing half a million Marks each. Moulds were built—each set costing the same amount again. But the plastics boom of the 1960s seemed to justify the investment. Using this technique, geobra produced floor gratings, ceiling plates, children's desks, toy grocery stores, ice hockey sticks and tennis rackets—even water-skis. The boss himself tested the latter—even training with the German national team in water temperatures of 50 °F.

The facilities in Zirndorf soon became too small. In 1969, factory and warehouse buildings were constructed in Dietenhofen in the district of Ansbach, 15.5 miles away. The first foreign-based production facilities followed in 1971: Brand Int. Ltd. and Inmold Ltd. were established on Malta. The new "factory" was just 27,800 sq. ft. in size, employed 60 workers and contained one injection moulding machine. Here, as in the main office, walkie-talkies, electronic telephones and toy grocery accessories were manufactured.

Malta had many advantages: The government provided the building, the rent was low, and so were the wages—approximately one-third of those paid in Germany. In addition, the location was much closer than the Far East, into which much of the competition was expanding.

A German success story

Up until the start of the PLAYMOBIL era, toy telephones remained one of the most important items in geobra's product line. Here, workers test and package Series 2990 models. For some time, however, the phones had already been intended to be more than toys: They could actually be used for in-house communication. For the Private Telephone 2000, connecting cables needed to be laid inside the home.

A German success story

Before appearing in cheerful publicity shots like this one, these colourful construction workers lived out a shadowy existence: The toy idea that Hans Beck developed in the early 1970s was initially given a low priority by his boss. Thus, the first prototypes languished in a drawer for some time.

DRAWER DESIGN AND FURNITURE PRODUCTION

Due to the competitive atmosphere in the toy sector, Brandstätter turned more and more toward non-toy products, even intending to begin producing furniture parts. He planned to offer ceiling panelling, plastic shelving, storage boxes and similar items via mail-order catalogue. But the 1970s brought the oil crisis. The oil-exporting countries of the Arab world were using their petroleum as a means of placing political pressure on Israel and its allies. Crude oil prices quadrupled, and plastic prices rose along with them. Simply acquiring sufficient raw material became difficult. Pressure from the competition was a further stressor, and the previously healthy family enterprise—which had always operated modestly and economically—suddenly found itself in the red and was soon on the verge of bankruptcy.

As early as 1971, Horst Brandstätter had given his head of development, Hans Beck, the assignment of creating a new product line. He was looking for a toy that would require less plastic and take up less room—in manufacturing, warehousing and shipping as well as on the now-crowded store shelves. The toy should have a system behind it, so that it would not be necessary to constantly invest enormous sums into mould-making and production. The idea was to win over new clients to the system with interesting expansion products and make them into regular customers for years to come. Brandstätter imagined a series of vehicles with accompanying figures. Up until that time, only Fisher-Price had produced similar little head-and-torso people. Beck sketched a few vehicles, such as trucks and postal vans with stiff-looking drivers. But with a boat, a hook-and-ladder truck and a bobsled, the figures became a significant element of the toy, and Hans Beck realised: "The figure is more important than the vehicle." His boss didn't quite agree at first. "All right," he supposedly commented initially, "you can keep working on it in your spare time." Thus, whenever he had a break between jobs, or the boss was not around, Beck pulled his prototype back out of the drawer. The figure was registered for a patent in Germany in 1972, and one year later in England, France, Italy and the USA. Over the course of three years, Beck constructed other products and developed accessories for the figures on the side. With the first test children—Beck's nieces and nephews—the little men were well-received.

In the early 1970s, Horst Brandstätter developed products such as furniture and office equipment, intending to sell them via mail-order catalogue. With the oil crisis of 1973–74—when raw plastic prices rose six-fold—the idea quickly faded from the scene. The only product that remained from that period was ceiling grating, which can still be seen in geobra's modern Zirndorf headquarters today.

A German success story

Placing the figures at the centre of the action was a revolutionary idea. The PLAYMOBIL system took on a high utility and play value through the constant development of new accessories, which were designed to fit the figures perfectly.

Horst Brandstätter put PLAYMOBIL on its feet.

CHRISTMAS STORIES AND OTHER MIRACLES

The crisis in the company came to a head. Shortly before Christmas 1973, the boss asked Beck if he could make the little men in his drawer presentable in time for the next Toy Fair in February 1974. With a lot of hard work, he was able to do so. At the fair, they were presented as a preview for the autumn 1974 product line, since the company had not even started production of the figures yet.

Sales partners showed practically no interest in the product until the second-to-last day of the fair, when the Dutch wholesaler Hermann Simon placed an order worth over one million Marks. The clever company head then used a trick to prompt German buyers to order PLAYMOBIL as well with the suggestion that one of the major companies was working to secure exclusive sales rights. Nobody wanted to miss out on a trend. As it turns out Brandstätter had almost gambled too high. The factory in Dietenhofen was equipped for a sales volume of one million; but more than three million Marks' worth of products had been ordered. New plastic injection machines needed to be brought in to keep up with the demand. But such machines could take as long as one year to arrive at the plant. Here, too, the company chief found a solution: "Through my connections, I got hold of a client list from Arburg, which at that time was the only manufacturer of the small machines we needed for our simple moulds. I called them one after the other, and asked if they would give up their used machines.

18

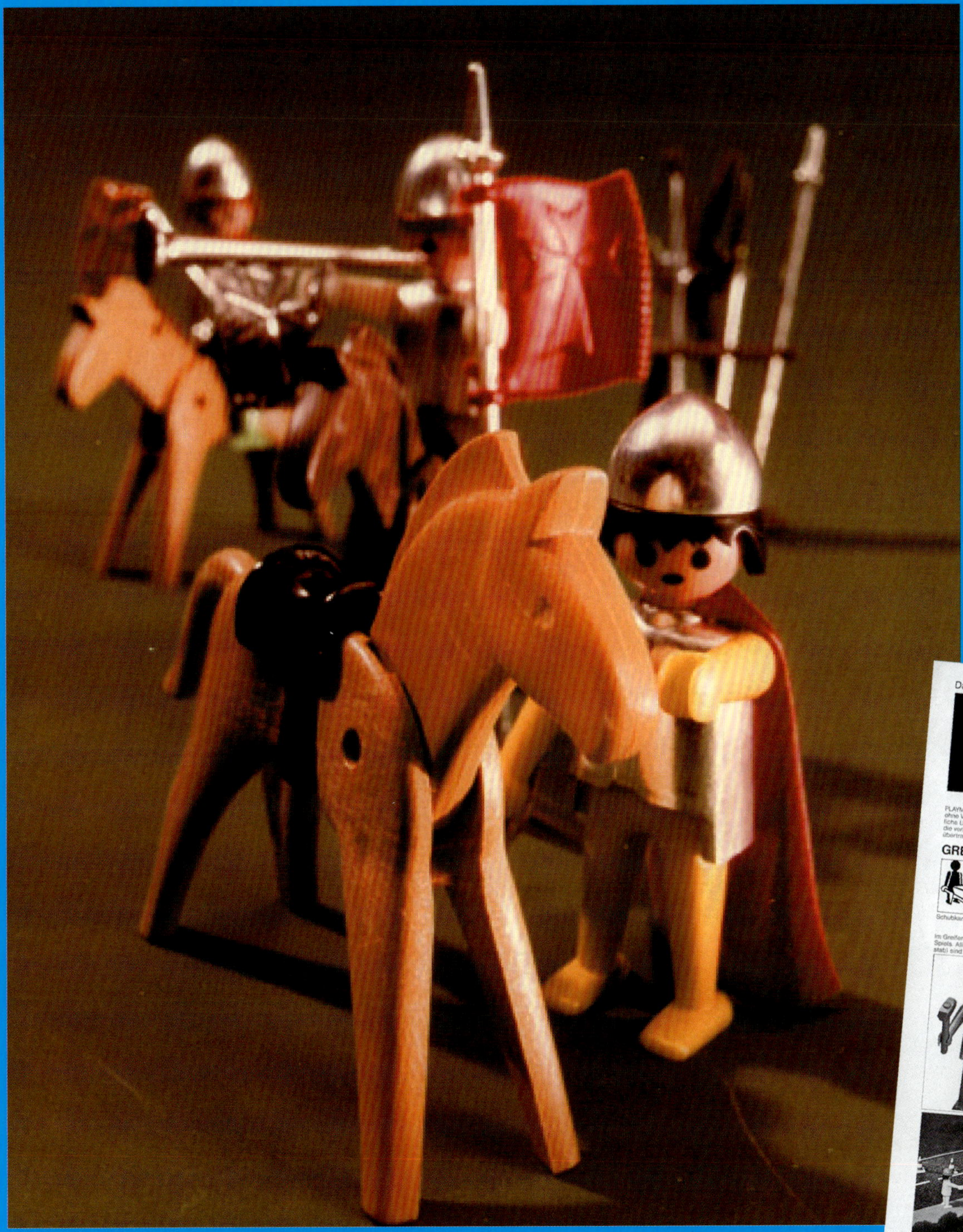

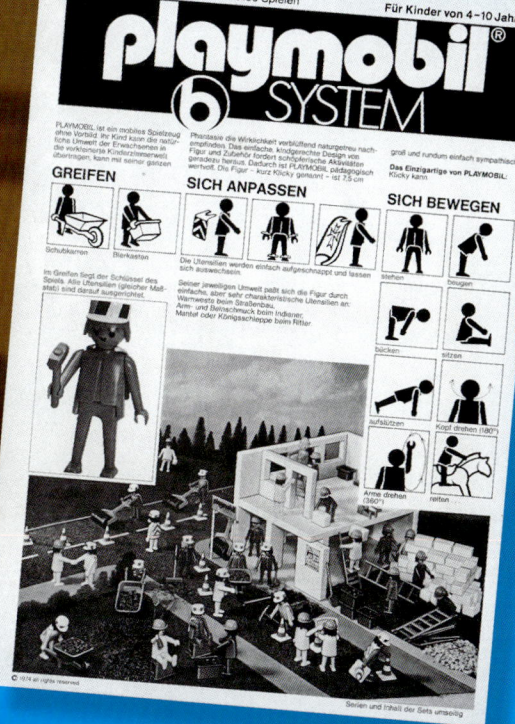

At the time of the market launch, horses appeared as the first animals in the PLAYMOBIL product line. When looked at from above, they have a wasp-like waist, which allows the PLAYMOBIL figures to ride them.

Das neue variable System für mobiles Spielen

Für Kinder von 4–10 Jahren

playmobil® SYSTEM

PLAYMOBIL ist ein mobiles Spielzeug ohne Vorbild. Ihr Kind kann die natürliche Umwelt der Erwachsenen in die verkleinerte Kinderzimmerwelt übertragen, kann mit seiner ganzen Phantasie die Wirklichkeit verblüffend naturgetreu nachempfinden. Das einfache, kindgerechte Design von Figur und Zubehör fordert schöpferische Aktivitäten geradezu heraus. Dadurch ist PLAYMOBIL pädagogisch wertvoll. Die Figur – kurz Klicky genannt – ist 7,5 cm groß und rundum einfach sympathisch.

Das Einzigartige von PLAYMOBIL: Klicky kann

GREIFEN

Schubkarren

Bierkasten

Im Greifen liegt der Schlüssel des Spiels. Alle Utensilien (gleicher Maßstab) sind darauf ausgerichtet.

SICH ANPASSEN

Die Utensilien werden einfach aufgeschnappt und lassen sich auswechseln.

Seiner jeweiligen Umwelt paßt sich die Figur durch einfache, aber sehr charakteristische Utensilien an: Warnweste beim Straßenbau, Arm- und Beinschmuck beim Indianer, Mantel oder Königsschleppe beim Ritter.

SICH BEWEGEN

stehen

beugen

bücken

sitzen

aufstützen

Kopf drehen (180°)

Arme drehen (360°)

reiten ...

Serien und Inhalt der Sets umseitig

Nowadays, every child knows what PLAYMOBIL figures can do. But in the beginning, information sheets were needed to explain the idea of the so-called "Klickys".

A German success story

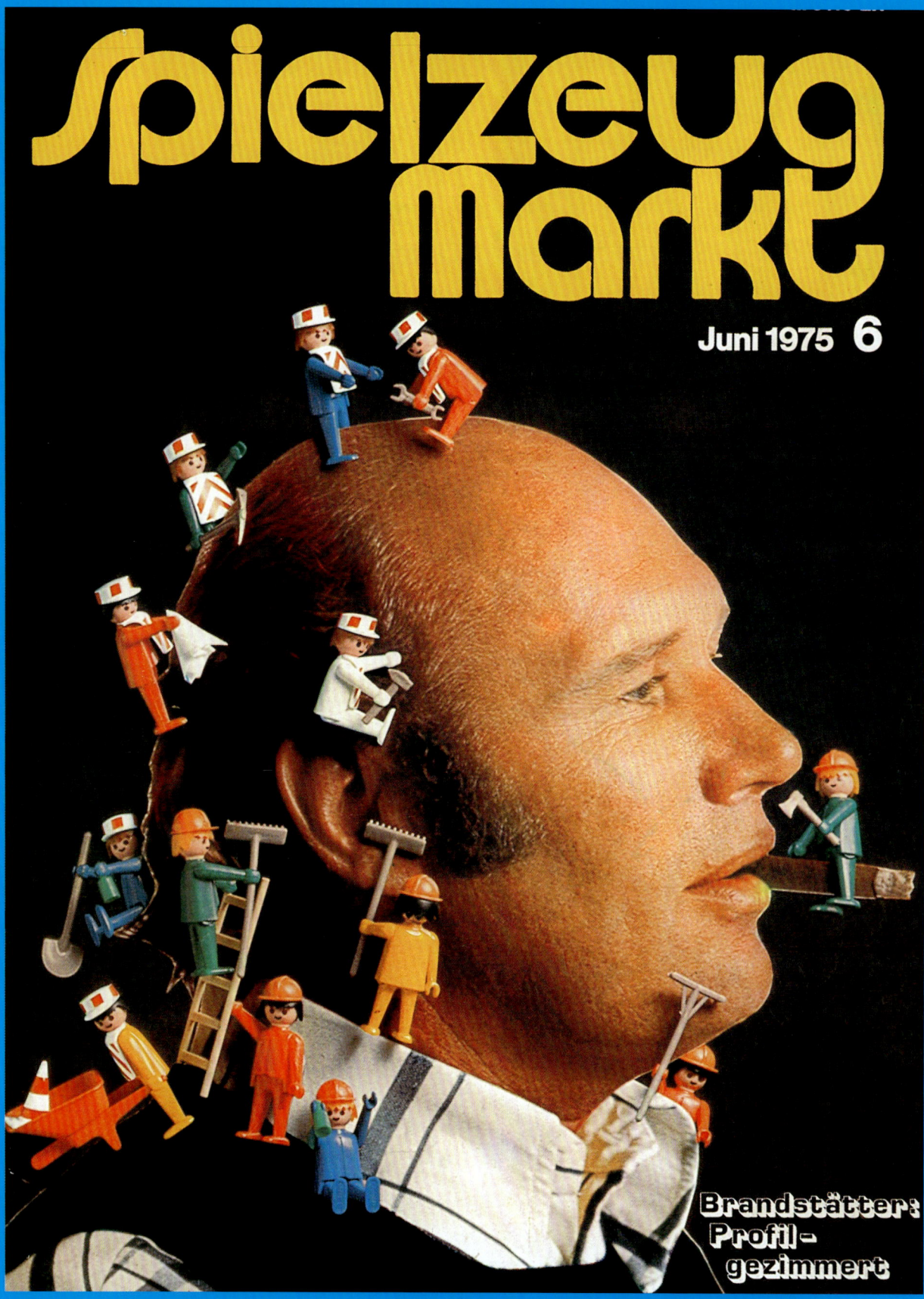

Just one year after its introduction on the market, PLAYMOBIL was already on course for success, and Horst Brandstätter was celebrated as a visionary in publications like this one.

Then we zipped around the country, picking up one machine at a time," said Brandstätter, remembering the difficult beginning. From then on, progress continued almost steadily uphill—all the way to the present day. In the first year, three million Marks' worth of PLAYMOBIL was produced; two years later, production had increased to 96 million Marks.

Within just a few years after the market launch, geobra Brandstätter had become the most profitable toy manufacturer in Germany, and it has remained so to this day. Of course, other companies witnessed PLAYMOBIL's success and tried to surpass it. As early as 1975, the BIG toy company in neighbouring Fürth—famous for its BIG Bobbycar—came out with PlayBIG figures, which were so similar in design and system concept that geobra went to court immediately. The regional and appellate courts decided in favour of geobra, and ruled that PlayBIG was an illegal imitation of the patented PLAYMOBIL. But the celebration in Zirndorf was short-lived. BIG took the case further, to the Federal Court, where the judges ruled "that PlayBIG figures have the look of a self-confident, athletic and aggressive young man, whereas PLAYMOBIL men have the appearance of a child—sweet and unsteady on his feet." So PlayBIG could continue to be produced. But the level of success was not what BIG had hoped for: Consumers chose PLAYMOBIL, and just a few years later, PlayBIG was no longer seen on store shelves. At geobra Brandstätter, on the other hand, the coffers were jingling. The profit from toy sales was 32 million Marks in 1975; one year later, it had reached 102 million.

Other companies also wanted a piece of PLAYMOBIL's pie. The PlayBIG figures from the BIG company (best known for its worldwide success with the Bobbycar) were the first and most formidable competitor, which Horst Brandstätter fought both in and out of the courts.

In the showroom, geobra was already ahead of development by 1975. In 1977, the first knights' castle and medieval buildings were added to the product line. In the same year, the little figures managed to jump the 100 million Mark profit hurdle.

HELP! EVERYBODY WANTS PLAYMOBIL

And the advertising began: TV spots, print advertising and other marketing methods aimed to make PLAYMOBIL well-known. And it worked. The toy shops placed orders, but they always received less than they asked for—geobra simply couldn't keep up. Only about half of the orders the company received could actually be filled. While the production department sweated, management practised writing letters of apology, all of which sounded more or less the same: "Dear customer, the demand for PLAYMOBIL systems exceeds all normal standards."

Complete orders could not be filled, so merchants were sent whatever products were available, "because the most important thing is that you have at least some PLAYMOBIL products to offer your customers," wrote then-head of distribution

A German success story

Geobra relied on print and television advertising from the very beginning. In November and December 1975, commercial spots ran on 35 early-evening programmes on regional television. In addition, there were radio spots and print campaigns in children's magazines such as Micky Mouse, Fix + Foxi, Felix and Bessy.

A German success story

PLAYMOBIL was a hit, and orders exceeded production capacity. Geobra employees worked day and night to produce enough of the little figures. Merchants were aware of the dire situation and doubled their orders to ensure that they would receive at least half as much.

Oswald Bayer, apologising to his clients in November 1976. Even the display department nearly broke down in despair: "We have been overrun by requests for display material. Unfortunately, we are not in a position to fulfil all of your wishes immediately," read an apology letter in October 1976. In fact, the problem of production squeezes in the period before Christmas can still occasionally occur today, especially in the case of new products. Then e-mails such as this one arrive in Zirndorf: "Before Christmas, jaw-dropping scenes were taking place in all the major cities in Germany. Parents, grandparents, nieces, nephews, aunts, uncles—everyone was looking for the jet airliner. Salespeople couldn't stand to hear it anymore, and they couldn't stand to say: The jet airliner is sold out."

A German success story

In 1978, stocking-up of children's rooms came to a temporary stop. Profits dropped for the first time, and the toy industry gloomily predicted PLAYMOBIL's impending end.

BIG INVESTMENT—
UNEXPECTED RESULTS

The delivery situation that started with the market launch crunch did not improve until 1977, when the boss invested 8.5 million Marks in moulds and machines. Soon all orders could finally be filled. But dealers, who had become used to receiving less than they requested, had been inflating their orders. Now, however, they received everything they wanted, and for the first time, a few blue boxes remained in the warehouse—an unusual situation for PLAYMOBIL. In the following year, 1978, sales went down for the first time. But by 1980, the company was already in the black again.

THE SUCCESS CONTINUES

The company was now investing enormous sums every year in increasing production. On Malta and in Dietenhofen, 270 fully automated injection moulding machines were in operation. In order to improve the delivery situation during the buying season, an automatically-controlled high rack warehouse was constructed in Dietenhofen, with room for 12,000 pallets; since 1992, the capacity has been increased to 28,000 pallets. Fears that the controlling equipment could one day break down were great initially, but by then, everyone knew that the company could not continue to exist without this storage facility.

By 1980, geobra's profit numbers had ascended to new heights. The Brandstätter Group achieved a revenue of 162.5 million Marks. In addition to geobra Brandstätter GmbH & Co. KG, the group also included the production facilities in Malta, the mould factories in Zirndorf and Malta, as well as HOB Electronics GmbH & Co. KG—the "baby" of Klaus Brandstätter, one of the boss's two sons—which developed video display terminals and compatible software. PLAYMOBIL's share of the profit pie was approximately 135 million. This means that on average, every German citizen bought 2.25 Marks worth of PLAYMOBIL. More than half of the little figures and their worlds were for export. They were especially popular in France, the Netherlands and Belgium, but also in Austria, Switzerland and other European countries. And in places where customs duties were too high, geobra allocated licenses to local firms that manufactured PLAYMOBIL in their own factories—for example, in Spain, the USA, Mexico and Brazil.

In the early 1980s, there were approximately 4,000 different PLAYMOBIL parts already in existence. In Dietenhofen, three million individual pieces were produced each day, and an average of 100,000 blue packages was readied for shipping. Anyone who has ever assembled a knights' castle knows how many individual pieces are included in each package. This means that at just the right moment, every one of these parts needs to be finished or available to go into the appropriate box.

In 1979, the blue-painted high rack warehouse was opened in Dietenhofen. Here, in a 367 feet long, 98 feet high and 95 feet wide space, rest millions of children's dreams. Only a computer knows which package can be found where. An emergency power unit ensures that even in the case of an outage, delivery will not need to be stopped.

A German success story

THE PLAYMOBIL IDEA TAKES HOLD

Now the concept behind the PLAYMOBIL system truly began to pay off. Not only was it easier for uncertain grandmothers, but it was also more economical to buy accessories for an already existing toy. How fortunate that PLAYMOBIL constantly offered new complementary products. Hans Beck made certain that the company's salespeople didn't get carried away with their financial success. Anything new that was added had to fit the product philosophy: no ostensible violence, no horror scenarios and no short-lived trends.

The toy industry was repeatedly amazed at PLAYMOBIL's on-going success. Even the company chief commented that PLAYMOBIL was "a product that we adults can't understand, because it is played out in the minds of children. As simple and unimpressive as the PLAYMOBIL items often seem to adults, they are exactly right for the children for whom they are intended."

After ten years of PLAYMOBIL production, 500 million little people already inhabited the earth. PLAYMOBIL's revenue was 182 million Marks. (Keep in mind, it was 3 million in the first year.) And progress was rapid. In 1981, Horst Brandstätter reported that the company had acquired a new IBM computer with 1 megabyte storage capacity. Three years later, the field staff was supplied with mobile data entry devices which could record orders by means of a bar code. Every evening, the orders were sent to the headquarters in Zirndorf via a postal service data network.

MARKETING PLAYMOBIL WORLDWIDE

PLAYMOBIL's popularity continued uninterrupted and applied equally to the entire product spectrum. Every year, new products were introduced at the Toy Fair. For each new item, an old one had to be removed from the assortment—if only for the simple reason that toy shops had a limited amount of shelf space available for the blue boxes. Thus, in 1985, only 18 new items were added to the programme, which included a total of about 180 items. Other ideas that the development department came up with remained in the drawer for the time being. The system—which was intended for children 4 to 10 years old—turned out to be a perennial hit. Even 11- and 12-year-olds still occasionally played with PLAYMOBIL. Now PLAYMOBIL increased its efforts to break into playrooms overseas. In Canada, an unusual promotional tactic was used: Esso service stations introduced a point system which promised a PLAYMOBIL Esso station at a low price when customers purchased enough litres of fuel. It wasn't quite as successful as Aral's point-collecting system for balls 20 years later, but nevertheless, 2.5 million PLAYMOBIL figures entered Canadian households in this way. A different promotional idea failed in the USA. In 1983, PLAYMOBIL figures were included in McDonald's Happy Meals. But the inexperienced American children had the bright idea to try to extend the figures' arms out to the sides. Since that was not their inventor's intention, the little

A German success story

people succumbed, their arms broke off, and the McDonald's campaign came to an early end. In general, Americans had a difficult time with PLAYMOBIL, and Toys 'R' Us tried to order only a few items from the line. But Horst Brandstätter said no—it had to be all or nothing. He knew, after all, that when a little PLAYMOBIL fan wanted a cowboy set, he would want that and only that. If his mother was unable to find it, she wouldn't buy a substitute, and there would be one less satisfied customer.

In the 1980s, the firm founded its own distribution companies in France, the Benelux, England, Italy, Canada, the USA and even Japan. The Japanese market turned out to be difficult too—Japanese children preferred playing with electronic games and home computers—and the distribution firm was dissolved again in 1988. In England, the toy with the not-so-foreign name also had a hard time. Founded in 1980, the marketing subsidiary did not record sizeable profits until five years later. Even though PLAYMOBIL was named "Toy of the Year"—and the industry praised the product, its field staff, on-time delivery and advertising strategy—sales did not take off initially.

In the early 1980s, customers at Canada's Esso service stations could collect points when filling their tanks. When you saved enough, you could take home your own PLAYMOBIL filling station. At the end of the campaign, 270,000 Esso stations and 2.5 million PLAYMOBIL figures had found their way into Canadian playrooms. Mission accomplished!

27

A German success story

NEW IDEAS ALONG THE WAY

In 1985, a new product sector joined the toys. Under the brand name Lechuza Strickwaren, the company tried its hand at heavy, hand-knitted traditional jackets decorated with pompons and embroidery. In the same year, the "Fiberline Bootsbau" brand was renamed "Modern Classic Yachts". This, however, did not alter the fact that the boats—to put it in simple business-speak—did not contribute to the overall revenue of the corporate group. Nor were the hand-knits a success. So the name Lechuza—which, by the way, means "owl" in Spanish—was transferred to self-watering plastic plant containers invented by Horst Brandstätter.

A NEW HOME FOR THE PLAYMOBIL MEN AND WOMEN

"First you need a good horse, and then a nice stable," thought Horst Brandstätter—and after about 15 years of PLAYMOBIL, he decided that the best horse in his stable was strong enough. At a cost of more than 50 million Marks, he built a new company headquarters on a green meadow in Zirndorf—a jewel of both form and function. Ever the chief, he left his personal stamp here as well—insisting, for example, on plastic ceiling panelling from geobra's 1970s product line. He saw his employees as his company's greatest asset. Consequently, in addition to spacious work areas, he included an employee health and fitness centre and a company childcare facility from the very beginning. Furthermore, the foundation was laid for the FunPark, which would officially open in the year 2000. At that time, it consisted of a 6,700 sq. ft. display area, PLAYMOBIL play corners and a gift shop.

On Malta, too, the facilities were bursting at the seams. After all, all of the figures were produced there (in 2003, they numbered over 70 million)— this was the piece which required the most manual labour and was much cheaper to produce on Malta than in Franconia. A new facility was considered, divided across several production

A German success story

PLAYMOBIL Land is no longer limited to children's imaginations: In the year 2000, the FunPark was opened next to the company headquarters in Zirndorf. Here you can find giant versions of all the PLAYMOBIL toys—from the pirate ship to the gold mine to the farm.

plants. In late 2002, production finally moved into the new 46,000 sq. yard complex near the airport. And in the Czech Republic, a new facility was added in the form of PLAYMOBIL CZ spol. s.r.o. Here, 100,000 so-called "preliminary bags" were assembled daily, which would then travel to outfit zoo, knights' castle or modern house packages in Dietenhofen.

A German success story

NEW TARGET GROUPS: PLAYMOBIL FROM THE GROUND UP

"The idea of our new product policy is not to constantly flood children's rooms with new items. Previously purchased and existing toys should take on extra value and remain attractive through the addition of new play possibilities. Long life cycles for PLAYMOBIL articles are thus an important goal." In 1987, PLAYMOBIL's name recognition was at 87 percent (compared to 67 percent in 1979); today it is at nearly 100 percent.

"For the last 15 years, we've been driving in the fast lane almost constantly. We're not so ambitious that we want to speed up business even more, but we have no intention of moving meekly back into the right lane," said the boss in the late 1980s as he considered new sales markets. PLAYMOBIL was still primarily a toy for boys, so in 1989, geobra introduced the nostalgic "1900" range, whose pink-toned package design clearly signalled that it was especially intended for girls. One year later, it was followed by the PLAYMOBIL 1.2.3 series, designed for children aged $1\,^1\!/_2$ years and up, with the aim of fostering brand loyalty early on. But the competition from other brands—such as Fisher-Price and LEGO Duplo—was still too strong. "1.2.3 is really a hard nut to crack. In this case, the adult customers' acceptance still leaves something to be desired." In 1993, the product was still struggling for recognition. And all in all, times were getting tougher—the economic slowdown was spreading. "Of course, a person who no longer has a steady income will think twice about putting another 150-Mark PLAYMOBIL toy under the Christmas tree," Brandstätter commented, "But we will not supply our PLAYMOBIL sets more meagrely just to make them cheaper, and there will be no reductions in quality." Instead, the lower-priced range was strengthened and more small sets were produced. Today, PLAYMOBIL is marketed in approximately 60 countries, and new products are introduced throughout the year: at the beginning of January, so children can invest their Christmas money well; in the spring—in time for Easter—so that the Easter bunny has something to bring. The third wave of new products arrives at summer holiday time, and in the autumn—at the start of the Christmas shopping season—come the fourth and the fifth. Since 1996, those who don't want to go shopping can order online: PLAYMOBIL has recognised the signs of the times and now occupies 500 pages on the World Wide Web.

The PLAYMOBIL 1.2.3 family.

A German success story

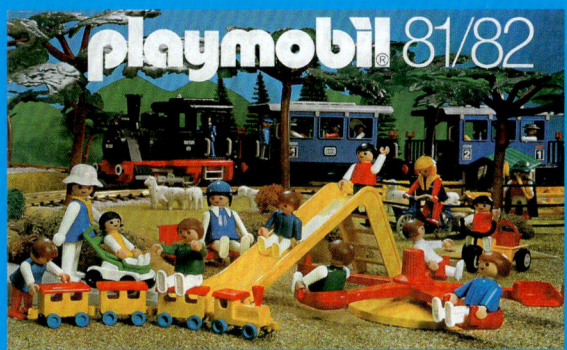

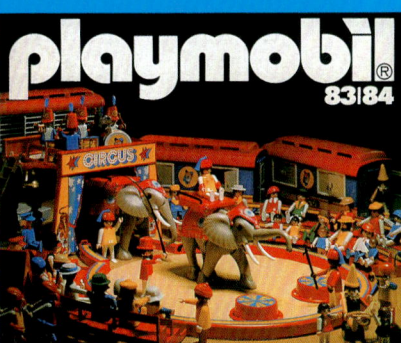
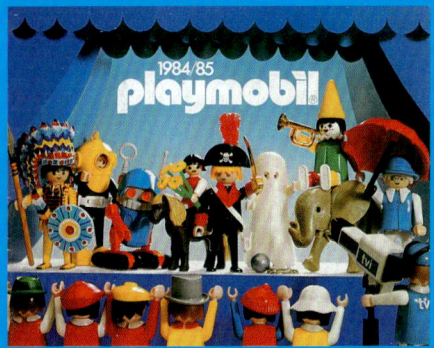

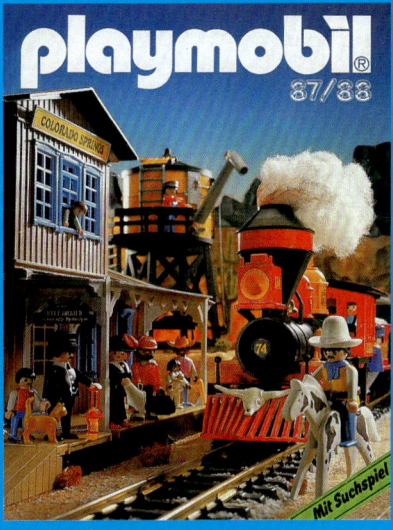
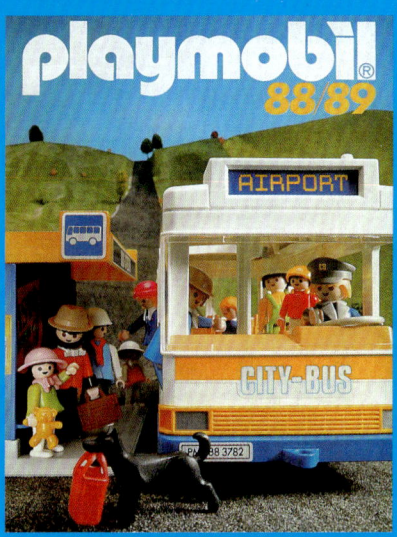

PLAYMOBIL catalogue title pages from the 1970s to 2004.

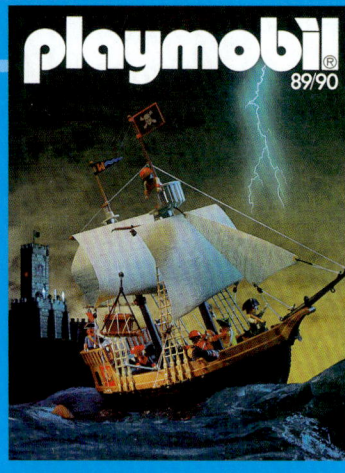
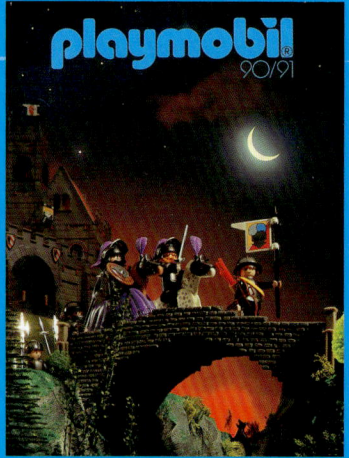
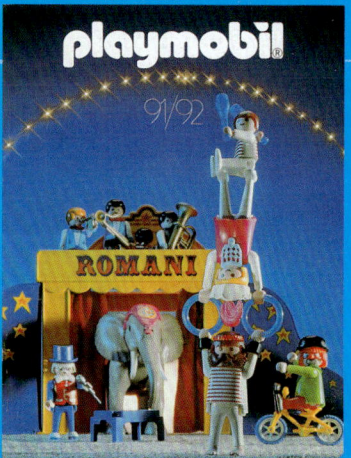
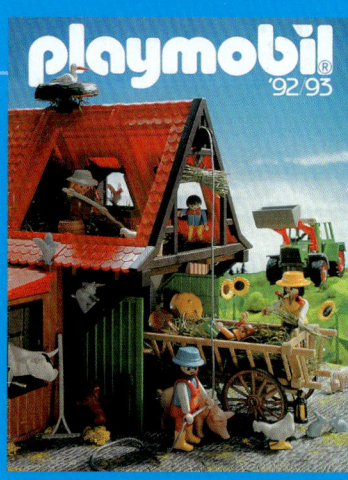
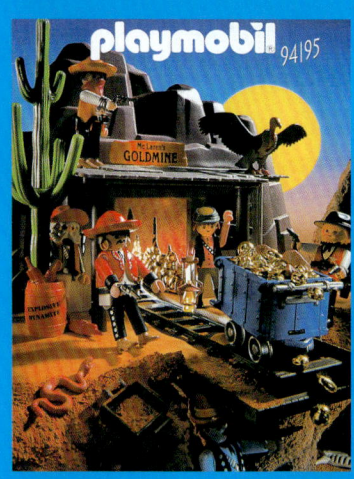

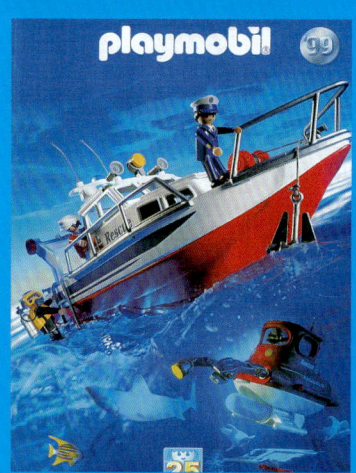
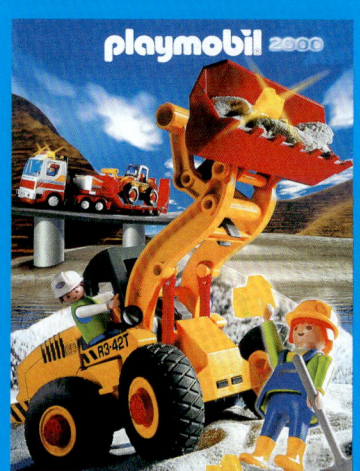
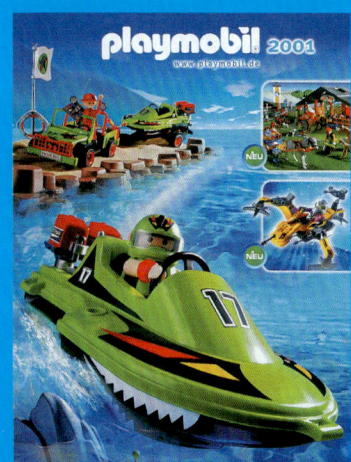

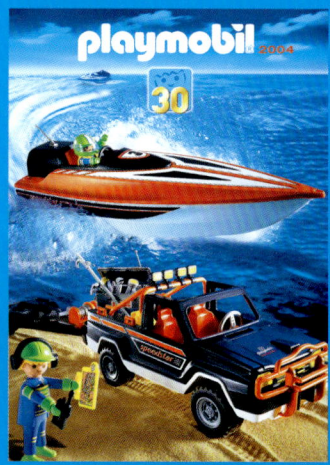

SMALL SETBACKS—GREAT OUTLOOK

Just in time for PLAYMOBIL's 25th anniversary, the company installed a new software system, which, unfortunately, did not report the season's orders to production on time. The result: Many Christmas wishes remained unfulfilled. Toy dealerships, parents and children were angry, and profits dropped for the first time since 1978—by 6.5 percent. But the firm entered the new millennium with renewed energy. In the year 2000, even babies were treated to their own PLAYMOBIL series, "First Smile for a smile from the start". And the SystemX Modern House updated the traditional dollhouse in children's rooms. Even though PLAYMOBIL values creative, self-directed play, the company followed fashion and introduced three computer games—with later versions for Gameboy and Nintendo.

At the turn of the millennium, the boss made provisions for his succession, and placed long-time employee Andrea Schauer in line for the throne. She is responsible for the development, marketing and sales departments. And since the early 1990s, in order to prepare geobra's workers for life without him, Brandstätter has been spending his winters in Florida—first, because it allows him to play golf in December, and second, to give him a chance to cultivate the American market, which has not yet succumbed to PLAYMOBIL mania. The clever businessman shies away from speculation; the idea of making his firm into a joint stock company would be terrible to him. Thus, he has provided for geobra Brandstätter GmbH & Co. KG to be integrated into the foundation "Kinderförderung von PLAYMOBIL" after his exit. Now it is up to Schauer and company to ensure that the firm's strategy is preserved: Since PLAYMOBIL's inception, it has been based on the continuous, long-term development of the product line and not on any short-lived trends. And this policy has paid off in the second generation: Parents who grew up with PLAYMOBIL themselves are aware of its quality and variety. Since the little people are nearly indestructible, children can also simply play with their parents' old collections.

The great-grandfather's casket fittings have grown into a genuine treasure chest. The 24 million Mark (approx. 12 million Euros) profit of 1974 had ballooned to 361 million in 2005. Nevertheless, this didn't all happen by itself: Geobra has invested over 600 million Euros since the product's market launch and has set new standards in many areas. Today, PLAYMOBIL represents a complete empire. Hans Beck's one-man development office has expanded into a 50-person development team. The machinery at the production facilities is always up to the newest standards, and the company prefers to train its employees on-site and cultivates a strong sense of community.

Dot, dot, dash— and the PLAYMOBIL face was done,
or how a little pencil drawing became a peaceful world power

Try this for yourself: Get one of the little people out of your children's room and take a good look at it. Small, easy-to-handle, and friendly, it faces you with open arms, ready for any game: helpful firefighter, creepy robber, simple train passenger, busy construction worker or shopping father. It is the prototype of a nice guy—one who can train horses as well as steal them. One who looks equally good in a police van or a getaway car. One who, admittedly, has a hollow head, but whose heart and soul are in the right place. One who can embody any character in a child's fantasy world. And a little over 30 years ago, it was something revolutionary.

PLAY WITH A SYSTEM

Children have always imitated the adult world in their play. But in the early 1970s, this impulse could only be partly realised. As far as toys were concerned, you could wish for a fire engine, but then you got a truck without people—or at most, small, stiff, plasticine men who remained stuck wherever you set them down on their platforms. But actually, a child wants to fight the fire and then get back in the truck and drive to the firehouse. Or on a construction site, to push the wheelbarrow aside and take a break. Even LEGO didn't have any figures of this kind in its product range at the time. PLAYMOBIL figures made a complete game possible for the first time. They can move, and above all, they can grab onto things: They can carry a stretcher as emergency medical workers; as construction workers, they can swing shovels and pick-axes, climb up a ladder or drive a vehicle back home. Just as the slogan said: "The PLAYMOBIL system—because one thing fits with another". From the very beginning, PLAYMOBIL was a toy with a system—and one which very nearly made just a single public appearance—at the Nuremberg Toy Fair in 1974. At first, nobody was interested in the little figures.

There were no comparable toys already on the market which could have hinted at their success.
One of the most important German toy buyers took Horst Brandstätter aside and said to him bluntly, "You've made a lot of good things. But this thing here is the biggest nonsense you ever put on the market." In Hong Kong, the buyer said, you could buy 100 figures for one Mark; a single PLAYMOBIL figure was supposed to cost two Marks. But on the second-to-last day of the fair, a miracle occurred: Hermann Simon from the Netherlands—the largest European toy wholesaler at that time—believed in the little revolution and placed the first order for PLAYMOBIL figures. Now Brandstätter's fighting spirit was aroused, and he did not shy away from making even personal sacrifices. The non-dancer dragged himself to the evening's Toy Fair ball in order to win over the managing director of VEDES, at that time the most influential toy dealership association. And his efforts paid off. VEDES placed an order. And when they heard of their competitor's interest, the department store chains Kaufhof and Karstadt did the same. Unlike the head buyers, children under-

To help children understand everything the figures can do, detailed instructions were included in the early packages.

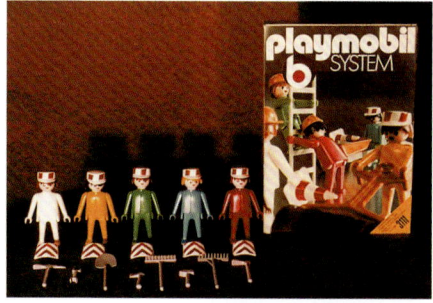
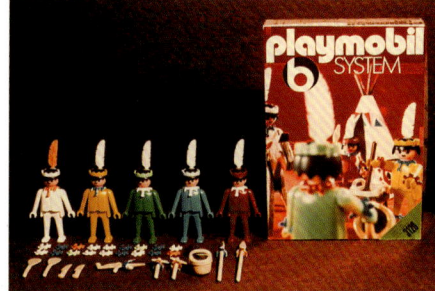

The first PLAYMOBIL men to come on the market were construction workers, knights and Indians. They exemplified the three areas still represented today: contemporary and historical play worlds and foreign cultures.

stood the concept immediately. The first assortment included construction workers, knights and Indians—something from the real world, from history, and from a foreign culture.

Nevertheless, sceptics in the trade remained: Even after PLAYMOBIL was posting double-digit profits every year, people continued to predict its imminent demise. But they were greatly mistaken: The PLAYMOBIL invasion was unstoppable. In 1990, after 16 years of PLAYMOBIL, the Badische Zeitung described its peaceful conquest as follows: "They've suddenly forced their way into children's rooms. They've made themselves comfortable in boxes and cartons. They came in droves, and there were more and more of them. Between mattresses, behind table legs, in the bottom shelves of closets—wherever there are holes, cracks or crevices, they make themselves at home. They came in fire engines, with excavators, and with pirate ships. In helicopters or TV broadcast vans. By water, by land or by air." And by now, a second generation is playing with them, mixing Mummy's and Daddy's figures together with the newer models.

Thanks to the "excavator gene" which frequently occurs in small boys—causing them to be fascinated by every sort of building site from infancy onwards—the construction workers were especially popular.

LITTLE DESIGN, BIG IMPACT

"The idea that every child is playing with it is still amazing," says Hans Beck, the father of PLAYMOBIL, more than 30 years after he sketched the little men for the first time. Born in Thüringen in 1929, the second oldest of nine siblings and half-siblings, he enjoyed playing with his father's treasures, a lead steamer and a warship—but he had to be very careful. A train didn't belong to him, either, but rather to his cousins, and it was something very special. So he made his own toys for himself and his siblings: "I had a weakness for tools—building and tinkering things myself," Hans Beck remembers. He was aided by a sturdy metal building kit (similar to the Märklin construction kits still known today). But even the genuine Hohstein "Kasperl" puppets that Santa Claus brought fascinated little Hans. In short, building and tinkering, as well as figures and role-playing, were subjects that were with Hans Beck almost from the cradle.

As a trained cabinet maker—who, instead of building furniture, was sent to work in the uranium mines—he fled Soviet-occupied Thüringen in 1948 and crossed the "green border" into Bavaria. Following various jobs in his field, the passionate model-builder came to geobra Brandstätter more or less by chance. In 1958, Horst Brandstätter was looking for a model maker for new products. But while all of the applicants were able to build models according to instructions, none was capable of developing his own. Hans Beck heard of the search through a fellow member of his model aeroplane club and was offered the job. He developed one of the model-building kits for V2 rockets and invented a "travel hula hoop" which could be dismantled into four parts and re-assembled as needed using plastic plugs. ("It wasn't a big success—it never really rotated in a smooth circle," he admitted openly, several decades later.) More successful was the tractor, first manufactured as a push-toy and later as a riding toy with pedals. Once again, geobra Brandstätter showed true inventiveness—as it did a short time later with its plastic piggy banks. "Before that there were only porcelain pigs, and you had to slaughter them. The plastic ones could be stuck, and later we also made them with keys," said Hans Beck, describing the innovation.

In the early 1970s, when geobra had already expanded to manufacturing modern office equipment and furniture made of plastic, an unfortunate turn of events made the raw materials too expensive. Hans Beck was asked to design a material-saving toy product in his spare time. His boss imagined a line of small toy vehicles for small children to push along, in the style of common wooden toys such as dump trucks and cranes. "Mr. Brandstätter said in passing that it would be nice to have a little man sitting inside," Hans Beck recalls. Thus, in 1971—with an idea and a few pencil sketches—a new era began in the world of toys.

The fat-bellied pirate captain (in 1986, the first figure with a tummy) is Hans Beck's personal favourite. In designing the animals, he aimed for a simplified, friendly appearance—which he achieved with great success. One of his last designs was the police officer's German shepherd.

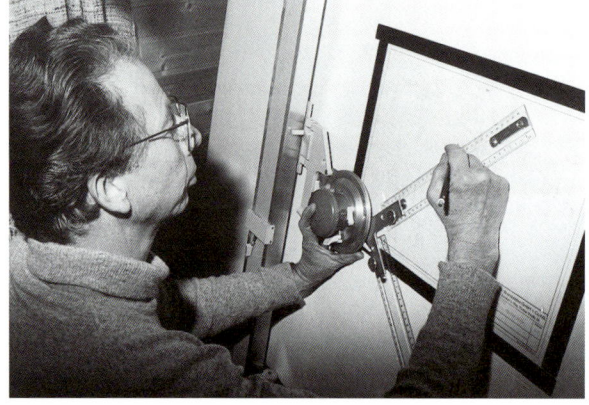

Geobra Brandstätter's old logo was the inspiration for Hans Beck's PLAYMOBIL face. The dot, dot, dash design has remained unchanged to this day.

Dot, dot, dash—

Dot, dot, dash—

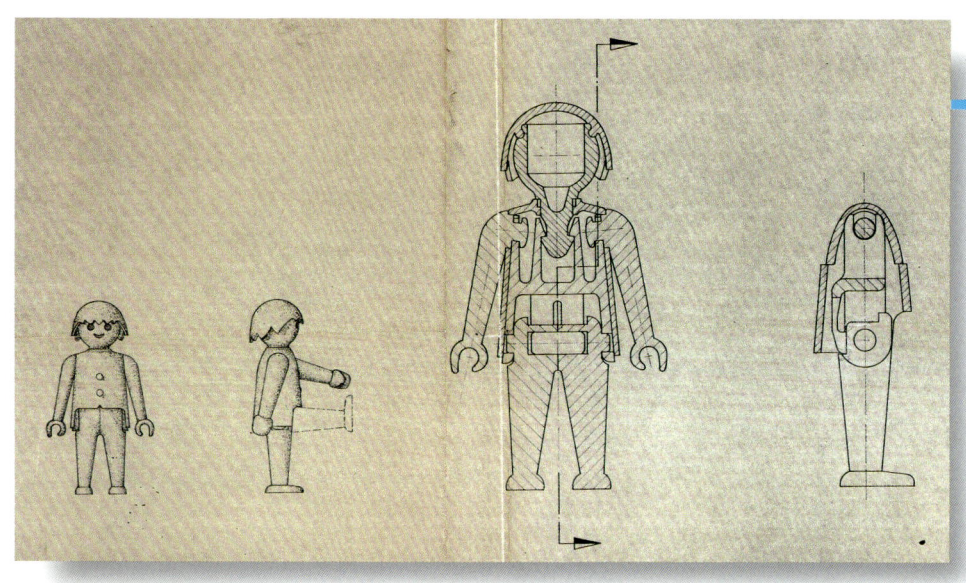

Right: In the design sketch for the patent application, the legs can still be moved separately; however, this detail was not put into practice.

Below: The classics—construction worker, knight and Indian—past and present.

IN THE DRAWER WITHOUT A NOSE

Rather than focusing on the cars, Hans Beck first turned his attention to their occupants. If the boss was imagining bowling pin-shaped figures à la Fisher-Price, Beck had completely different ideas: "I wanted to make something that was more interesting and versatile to play with. That meant that the figure should have a movable head, movable arms and legs, and the ability to hold things in its hands." He carved and assembled the prototype—at first with a nose, but that seemed too clownish to him. "That limited the figure so much; and I thought that the child's fantasy should determine the character," said the inventor. So the next attempt was made without a nose, with the friendly face that still smiles today as it did more than 30 years ago: Dot, dot, dash, and the PLAYMOBIL face was done.

But it was not as simple as that: Hans Beck tested several hand-painted versions before he settled on the final face, which has the appearance of a pictogram. It was based to some degree on the geobra brand logo at that time. After the failed attempt with the plastic nose, he gave up on that idea entirely. There are no existing versions with painted-on noses, either. The figures are meant be as simple as possible, so as not to inhibit a child's imagination. The proportions, too, are rather childlike. When asked to name his inspirations, Hans Beck could only think of one comparison: Charles M. Schulz's Peanuts characters—figures who looked like children but had adult problems.

When Horst Brandstätter came by, Beck presented him with the figures he had constructed up to that point. "I showed him what the figure could do: stand, sit, hold things, turn its head." Despite his initial scepticism, Horst Brandstätter permitted his model maker to continue working on the project during slow periods. As a precaution, the little men were also soon registered for a patent. The highly technical-sounding description in the patent application—"Toy figure with body open at the bottom whose arms and legs are secured with a bearing inserted through the body and attached to the head, and which can be moved in opposition to the body at each socket"—was, to begin with, a fabrication. Based on the first drawings, the proportions, head and movements were developed for the hand-carved prototypes of the figure. So Beck continued to work on his invention. Whenever he had time, he pulled it out of the drawer and tinkered around with it. By the end of the summer of 1971, he had seven hand-assembled figures in front of him, and he began designing tools for them. "I first thought of knights and Indians, and then of construction workers—children are familiar with them. I soon added the first vehicle, a little car," the inventor recalls. "Then I gave them to the children of neighbours and relatives whenever I had the chance." And from what he then observed, Beck was convinced that his invention was a good one. The test children played with the toys with rapt attention, developed relationships with them, and demanded more.

Dot. dot. dash—

The first sketches of the world-famous figure, still with a nose. But this only ever existed on paper, and later as an accessory for the circus clown. Clearly recognisable from the beginning was the characteristic zigzag haircut.

"The figure that I designed was an impressionistic model of a human figure. I tried to make it as simple as possible, in order to give free rein to every child's imagination." Hans Beck, 1976

Hans Beck's first five handmade models with painted-on faces. An angry PLAYMOBIL figure was also considered in the beginning.

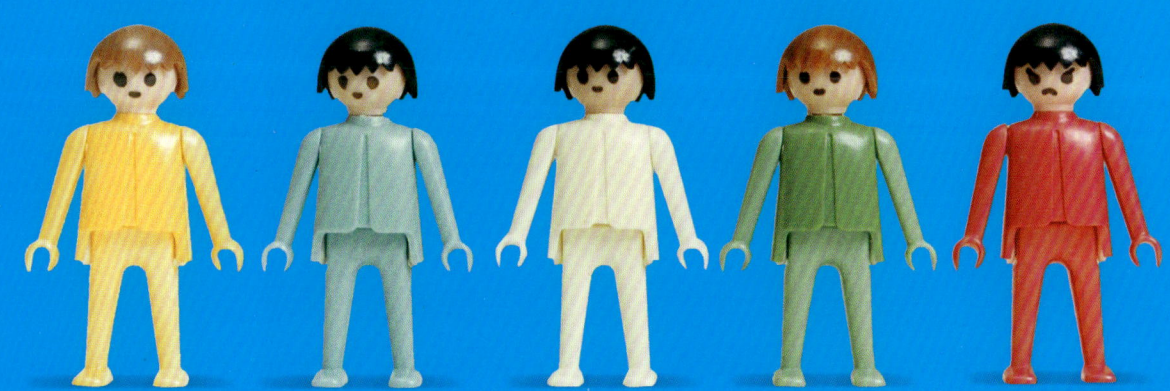

ROUND HEAD, STURDY LEGS AND THE RIGHT SIZE

It looks simple, but it's been precisely thought out. The ingenious inventor took his cue from children's drawings, in which the heads are generally round and disproportionately large. The facial expression should not portray a specific emotion, since the figure enters the world in a neutral state. Only a few accessories—a feather on its head, a hard hat or a knight's helmet—give the character an identity. Developing the right wig design was no easy task. In the beginning, the hats didn't stay on the hair: Thus, a figure could either have just hair or just a hat—which did not look very attractive. But here, too, Hans Beck experimented until he came up with a ridge that encircled the head and onto which any head covering could be snapped. The hands were a much more difficult problem, since they needed to be able to properly hold everyday objects such as bottles and brooms, but should also be able to grip a bow and arrow. The hands were also intended to swivel from the very beginning—but in this case, the injection moulding technology had not yet advanced far enough. Therefore, the first generation of figures had single-coloured arms and legs which were manufactured in one process step. Since 1981, the hands have been flesh-coloured, and they can finally be rotated. Knee and elbow joints would have made the figures less stable, and their appearance would have been too technical—so Beck decided against them. A PLAYMOBIL figure is exactly 2.9 inches tall and fits well in a child's hand. The scale of 1:24, based on the length of the figure, makes it possible to fit the whole PLAYMOBIL world into a child's room.

In the beginning, testimonials from educators and psychologists were used to convince parents of the value of PLAYMOBIL.

Dot, dot, dash—

In September 1981, offspring finally arrived in the PLAYMOBIL family. The child figures are 0.78 inches smaller than their parents are; however, the inner surface of their hands is identical, allowing them to hold every accessory.

Over the years, developers have elaborated on the figures more and more, adding such details as freckles and hair ribbons.

43

Dot. dot. dash—

THE RIGHT SHOE SIZE AND THE RIDING PROBLEM

The legs—which, according to the patent application, were designed to move separately—stand stiffly side by side. "We noticed that children move the figures around as a whole, like board game tokens, and don't move the legs in a walking motion," said Hans Beck, explaining this development. The proper shoe size was also a question of millimetres. How big did the feet need to be to make the figures stable enough; and how small could they be to fit in aesthetically with the overall look? And then there were the horses—the people should be able to ride on them. Thus, in 1971, Hans Beck designed a rider figure with a wide stance. But this was too specialised: "The bow-legged construction worker didn't look right on the scaffolding," he recalls. Instead, the stance was widened only slightly, and the horses were given a wasp-like waist in order to provide room on their backs for both saddle and rider. Up until this time, Beck had been tinkering away on the figures by himself. Shortly before Christmas 1973, the boss came to see him: "On December 15, Mr. Brandstätter asked me: Do you think we

can get the figures ready in time for the fair?" Beck thought the schedule was too tight. It was only six weeks until the Nuremberg Toy Fair, with Christmas in between, and he would be working on it all alone. But Beck sat down at his desk; he was aware of the company's troubles and he had to think of his own position. He was on his own: He had to decide how to produce them in series and how to package and present them. Fortunately, the boss was already willing to spend

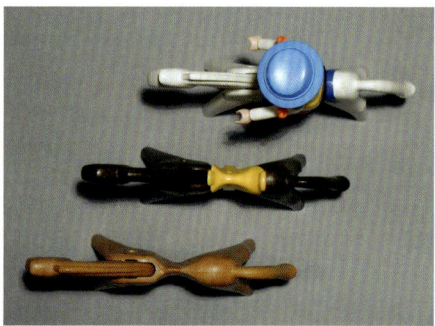

To allow them to carry both saddles and PLAYMOBIL figures (without specially-widened legs) on their backs, the horses were given wasp-like waists.

35,000 Marks to have a complete set of moulds built. It was not suitable for mass production, but it would be good enough for the samples. Practically enough, the little men fit into see-through packages similar to those used for card games. Beck constructed presentation platforms in the company's model room. Once the decision was made to present the little people at the Toy Fair, the question came up, "So what are we going to call them?" "The syllable 'play' is well known in the world of

Working overnight, Hans Beck also built the backdrops for the first presentation on the company premises in 1974 and experimented with the packaging.

toys, and Mr. Brandstätter considered a few ideas such as 'plaything', 'mobil play', 'play mobil'. I said PLAYMOBIL sounds better—use that one."

The name needed to be understandable worldwide from the very beginning, since the company had always produced many products for export. And then in February 1974, it was time: The PLAYMOBIL men were presented in geobra Brandstätter's sample room parallel to the Toy Fair. The rest is history…

Dot. dot. dash—

"I haven't lived for nothing," said Hans Beck, the father of PLAYMOBIL—honoured here by Horst Brandstätter—upon retiring in 1998 after 40 years at geobra Brandstätter.

And there was no stopping it: Thanks to Hans Beck's ideas, Horst Brandstätter's uncompromising willingness to take risks and the children who loved the first play system to put the figures at the centre of the action from the very beginning. The few sample figures did not remain alone for long. Hans Beck and his rapidly-growing development team designed entire play worlds. Animals, vehicles, buildings and lots of accessories were added—all perfectly matched to the figures in scale and design. Not only did the PLAYMOBIL empire grow to its present population of 1.7 billion, but by now, second and third generations are playing with old and new PLAYMOBIL toys, and the collectors' community comprises an estimated 5,000 members worldwide.

Hans Beck remained at geobra Brandstätter for a total of 40 years. Not only was he the inventor and father of the PLAYMOBIL figures, but since the product's market launch, he became, so to speak, the conscience of the corporation. When he retired at the age of 69, his development team—which by then had grown to 50 workers—had long since internalised his philosophy and would continue his life's work. Short-lived trends, horror and violence are not to be found in the PLAYMOBIL assortment. "We don't want to communicate a specific image to the children. We are giving them a toy with which they can play freely, and every child will use it differently," said Hans Beck, explaining his idea for the system of toys that revolutionised the playroom. In addition to his official retirement celebration, Beck received letters of thanks from fans large and small—all of whose childhoods would have been quite different without PLAYMOBIL.

"It was May 19, 1976, my fifth birthday. Out of the flood of presents which washes over a five-year-old, my uncle's gift stood out clearly: It was a plastic package with little compartments out of which little plastic men were grinning, with some kind of funny plastic accessories all around them. I would be lying if I said that I knew what to do with that jumble of plastic. But after a little time and repeated tries at sticking things together, I came to the surprising conclusion that these must be construction workers. And in fact, they were little masterpieces of toy-making: completely movable, functional from hard hat to wheelbarrow—and they looked good, too. And their happy smiles had me convinced for some time to come that construction workers are always in a good mood on the job. This is more or less how it was with my first—really my very first—package of PLAYMOBIL. In the years to come, my parents would have to pay dearly for what my uncle had started with nothing but good intentions. Because the more play ideas that were moulded into plastic—the more the PLAYMOBIL assortment grew—the more strongly my passion was aroused. Construction vehicles, cowboys, knights' castles, framework houses—I acquired a very respectable collection. And after years of puberty-related neglect, my friendly little figures experienced a Renaissance. Just as other people collect stamps, coins or toilet covers—at the age of 25, I was seized by a childish mania and became a PLAYMOBIL collector."

Elmar Schön, editor of the ZDF Heute Journal, wrote these words of reminiscence in honour of Hans Beck's retirement in April 1998.

Dot, dot, dash—

The little man from 1974 has gone on to populate an entire world. Whereas the first large sets were just cars and figures—nowadays, almost anything is possible. The figures even have their own circus.

47

From the development desk to the toy counter—three years of work

Hans Beck's one-man development division grew—like the product's success—at a rapid rate. First a draughtswoman was hired; six months later, the team had increased to five people. Today—more than 30 years later—a group of 50 employees works on developing new products. They are primarily industrial designers and model builders, but also trained mould makers—and yes, even sculptors. But the most important job criterion remains the instinct for play.

Behind closed doors

A trained window dresser, Bernhard Hane joined PLAYMOBIL in 1977. After many fruitful years as head of the display department, he stepped into Hans Beck's shoes. Since 1998, he has headed the development department, where new heart's desires are constantly being created. However, the company also reworks existing subjects—and, if necessary, updates them.

"Really, we're all big kids," says Bernhard Hane, head of PLAYMOBIL's secret development department. Behind security-coded doors, the team develops the products that will become coveted Christmas wishes up to three years later. The creative workers take their inspiration from the suggestions of hundreds of PLAYMOBIL fans, large and small, from whom they receive ideas, wishes and drawings every day; from observing their own children and their friends; and sometimes simply from their own unfulfilled childhood longings. Thus, the Tree House (item 3217), which was introduced in 2003, was an idea that one of the "big" boys at PLAYMOBIL had dreamed of for a long time. Of course, the developers also expand upon the existing play worlds—one example, being the case of the construction site in autumn 2003. Unlike in real life, where the building sector constantly complains about a lack of contracts, there is no recession in sight at PLAYMOBIL. What started as a few construction workers with pick-axes and a wheelbarrow has grown into the P&M contracting firm, expanded to include the crane and cement mixer that many fans have long wished for. Likewise, the Construction Trailer (item 3207) from 1976 has evolved into today's Construction Crew's Office (item 3260) with a bathroom, loft bed, desk and mini kitchen.

Behind closed doors

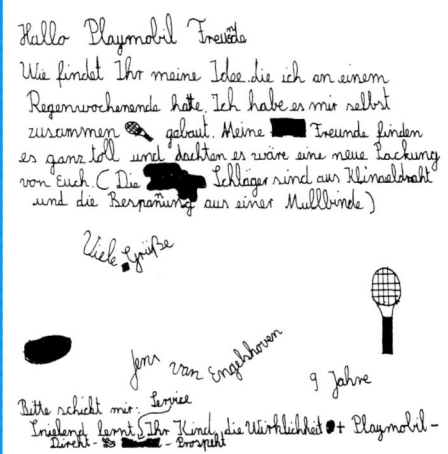

Every day, the PLAYMOBIL-makers receive suggestions and wishes from little fans for items they long for in the PLAYMOBIL assortment. In cases where the suggested items have appeared on the market a few months later, some people have tried to claim a share of the profits. However, an idea has generally been in the works at PLAYMOBIL for three years before the toy is available for purchase.

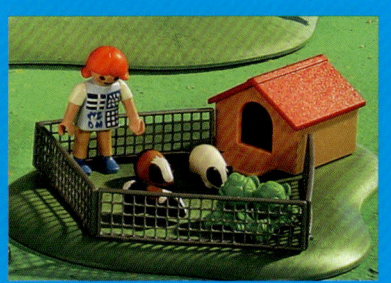

Behind closed doors

HOW DINOSAURS FINALLY CAME TO PLAYMOBIL AFTER 30 YEARS

Some ideas were considered for a long time before developers thought of a way to put them into practice. Thus, for example, the Noah's Ark, which arrived on the market in 2003, had been under discussion for some time. Hans Beck remembers: "The theme is an old one, and it's been suggested many times, but the size was always a problem—it would have been such a monster. We managed to wriggle out of the problem by using baby elephants; it wouldn't have worked with the big ones." Similarly, children had suggested a dinosaur theme over and over throughout the years. But two arguments had always stood in the way: On the PLAYMOBIL scale, a dinosaur would be quite large and would require a great deal of material. Furthermore, it wouldn't fit in with the philosophy, "because one thing fits with another", since dinosaurs and humans didn't even exist at the same time. But in the toy's anniversary year, a satisfactory solution was found for this problem as well. In January 2004, Professor Rasmussen and his team discovered frozen dinosaur babies, preserved in PLAYMOBIL ice. Gone were the problems with time travel and disproportionate sizing. Other wishes could not be realised for economic reasons. "PLAYMOBIL products are intended to be marketed worldwide. If we get a letter that says, '[the North Sea island of] Helgoland needs a fishing cutter,' it's certainly attractive to children living on Helgoland or on the coast, but children in the USA won't be terribly interested," explains Bernhard Hane. In the same way, the frequently-expressed wish for a THW (Technisches Hilfswerk—a German federal disaster

In 2003, the ark appeared—made possible through Noah's trick of inviting only the baby elephants. The dinosaur theme was also finally realised in the anniversary year, once the time problem had been solved by means of a discovery "preserved in ice".

52

Behind closed doors

relief organisation) fleet was rejected as too Germany-specific. "Of course, it would be simple to produce blue travelling cranes and vans and print the logos—but in France and the Netherlands, the Technisches Hilfswerk doesn't exist. And it wouldn't pay off for the German market alone," says the development head matter-of-factly.
Even during Hans Beck's time, there were nice ideas that either couldn't be realised or did not sell very well. Produced only as a prototype and never mass-produced was a beautiful Mississippi steamboat that graced Beck's workshop in Zirndorf for many years; it would have fit in beautifully with the Western theme... Other ideas were produced, such as the winter sports theme package in the 1980s: Children liked it, but it was not really appropriate as a year-round item.

Eskimos and winter sports were in the programme only for a short time. There were too few possibilities for expanding on the theme—and it was not necessarily a toy for all year round. Nowadays, sleds and snowmen continue to appear regularly in the Advent calendars.

Behind closed doors

"The Arctic theme was also nice, but it wasn't a hit. Maybe back then (1985) it was still too far away for the children," said Hans Beck, reflecting on the possible reasons for its failure. Nowadays, when we have The Little Polar Bear, it would surely be better received."
Cowboys have also disappeared from the assortment, at least for the time being. Only an Indian village, a covered wagon, bandits and a sheriff with three cowboys (available via the direct service catalogue) remain as reminders of the glorious days when PLAYMOBIL wrote Wild West history. But the zeitgeist doesn't stand still in the toy world, either. Whereas the children of the 1970s grew up with Winnetou, Bonanza and The Virginian, Western films no longer have the same presence in today's media.

Other articles remain perennial winners—such as the pirate ship or the knights' castle, which are among the top-selling products. Of course, they are constantly being updated, but many of the basic forms remain the same, and are simply redecorated or combined in new ways.

Cowboys rode into PLAYMOBIL's world as early as the 1970s. In those days, children grew up with Bonanza, The Virginian and The Waltons. Nowadays, the Western theme is only popular for dressing-up holidays such as Carnival or Halloween, and thus is barely represented in the PLAYMOBIL assortment.

Behind closed doors

"We didn't dare to attempt a jet airliner for a long time, because it would have been too big and therefore too expensive. Finally we mustered our courage and took it on. Of course we had to make concessions. It can only seat one person on the right side and one on the left, but that's enough to play with."
(Bernhard Hane)

BIG KIDS WITH MORE AND MORE IDEAS

Every year, there are approximately 60 new items in the programme—ranging from a large set for 150 Euros to Special figures for just under two Euros. From the first idea to the store shelves, development can take up to three years.
Take, for example, the circus theme. "Before we even start to work, we discuss the theme with the sales and marketing departments," explains creative chief Bernhard Hane. "Once the idea is accepted, we discuss the individual items. What does a circus need? A circus needs a ring—that's one item. A circus needs a circus wagon, a tractor and animals and acrobats. Now the structure starts to develop. We talk about these items," says Hane, describing the work prior to actual development.
At the very first discussion of a theme, the team considers how many items should be included in the series and whether they should all come onto the market at once or in two stages. Then they finally start to work...

Behind closed doors

The circus is one of the themes for which a number of items are planned. Animal, performer and vehicle sets expand on the large basic package.

Behind closed doors

"NEW-NEW" IS THE MOST FUN TO MAKE

"Of course, we're also eager to do something completely new—something 'new-new', so to speak. But the subjects that we haven't touched at all in the course of over 30 years are very limited," muses Hane, a native of Westphalia. The structure of the product line is simple: PLAYMOBIL covers both contemporary and historical themes. "There is still a lot of potential as far as history is concerned. So we have to consider whether the subject fits into the assortment at all and whether it doesn't encroach on another theme," says the development head, thinking in practical and sales-oriented terms.

The Beauty Salon was among the new products introduced in 2004.

The Grocery Store was at the top of many wish lists during the Christmas 2002 season. At PLAYMOBIL, it falls into the category of "girls' subjects"—but of course, it's also appropriate for brothers and other boys.

Behind closed doors

THE LONG ROAD TO THE PLAYROOM

Once an idea is accepted, there are many steps to cover before the product is packed in its blue box. In the case of the tree house, for example, the designers reached into their big PLAYMOBIL chest and built the first model using many parts that already existed—such as tree trunks, rocky landscapes and a log cabin; then they began developing it further. Brand new ideas are first sketched on paper. Here, developers may be helped by examples in books, actual models—or by visiting a construction site, as in the case of the crane. But the accessories are never exact scale models of any real examples. "We make an effort to design the things we develop in such a way that they fit with our greatly simplified figures and allow the child's fantasy plenty of room to play," said Hans Beck, explaining the product philosophy early on. And his successor, Bernhard Hane has continued in the same spirit. The development head patiently explains the green Economy Car (item 3069): "Naturally, it would have been easy to build an imita-

The above is the Smart car; to the right is the PLAYMOBIL economy car. The similarity is intended, but it is not a direct copy.

tion of a Smart car. But the real artistry lies in designing the car so that it doesn't seem quite real, but doesn't look cartoon-like either. Everyone can decide for himself what he sees in it."

Now the exact design drawings follow—including the precise number of parts from which the car, dinosaur or vacuum cleaner will be made—and the first carved prototypes, the so-called hand models. If everything looks the way it should in the finished toy, the models or drawings are scanned, digitized and passed on to the company's own mould makers or to an outside firm. Constructing the injection moulds from hundredweight stainless steel blocks can take up to four months. First, a rough form of the PLAYMOBIL piece that will later drop out of the mould is manufactured. It is made from graphite, like the tip of a pencil, and is very fragile. It serves as a template for the mould, with all of its details. In precise, laborious work, the steel is milled out, drilled and cut to form the shape that will later be injected with liquid plastic. A finished mould can weigh up to two tons. Particularly complicated moulds are those used for two-, three- or four-coloured parts, which will be manufactured in one process step using one

The hundredweight injection mould is installed in the injection moulding machine. This one is for manufacturing dragon feet. A computer controls the quantity that drops out of the machine every day.

Behind closed doors

THE PLAYMOBIL PEOPLE'S PARTS WAREHOUSE

On the ceiling-high shelves that line the walls of the development department, all the individual parts for every imaginable PLAYMOBIL figure are stored. For example, there are 100 different drawers containing arms: There is a purple left arm, a green short-sleeved right arm, children's arms in every colour of the rainbow, single-coloured arms and bent women's arms. Behind them, on a sliding shelf, you can find hairstyles of every kind; next to these are 50 different click-on cuffs. When a new figure needs to be created, the designers first look in these drawers and then pick up a printed slide to prepare a fashion show containing 20 different outfits. Anyone who walks past the desk gives his or her opinion, until the choice is down to just two or three figures. Then a team from the marketing and sales department makes the final decision as to what, for example, the grocery store uniform for the produce saleswoman should look like.

machine—such as the chimpanzees, the PLAYMOBIL babies, geese or cows. The moulds used to make the spotted cow family (bull, cow and calf) cost a total of nearly 800,000 Euros. Over 6,000 steel injection moulds, valued at around 300 million Euros, are now stored in a high-security room at the production plant. On an average, 300 new moulds are added every year.

The stuff of which a million children's dreams are made: Giant silos store the plastic granules which will be cast into figures, vehicles, animals and individual parts with a permanent shape, colour and play value.

TOY PARTS IN A THOUSAND VARIATIONS

When the moulds are finished and the first trial castings have come out well, production can begin. Gigantic silos stand outside the gates of the production plant in Dietenhofen. Each of the 17 towers holds 60 tons of plastic granules— approximately 7000 tons are used each year. The charming labels, such as "old town grey" or "creamy white", let the observer imagine what could be made out of them. A system of pipes automatically transfers the granules to the appropriate moulding machines. Over 200 state-of-the-art injection moulding machines stand in row after row in Dietenhofen, including numerous two-, three- and four-colour machines. This is also one of the secrets of PLAYMOBIL's

Behind closed doors

Several baby torsos are cast simultaneously in a single process step. In four colours, with a swivelling head and movable arms, they drop out of the bottom of the machine. The leg sections are cast in a neighbouring machine and later snapped onto the bodies by hand.

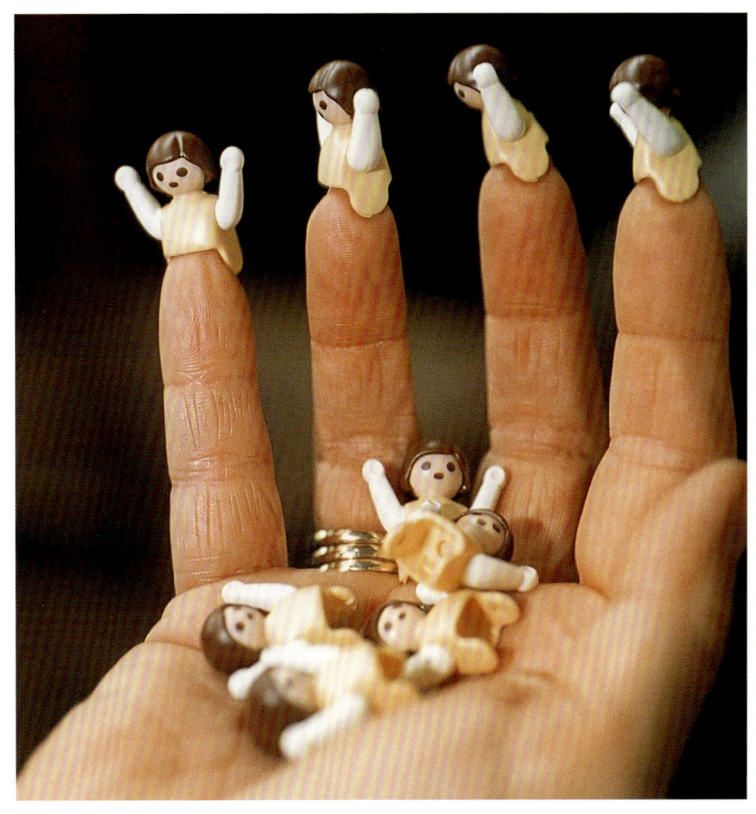

success. No corners are cut as far as the machinery is concerned. "This is another reason why the company was successful. We participated in every phase of technical development. Starting at a relatively low level, it has grown with every passing year," says Hans Beck, accurately assessing the company's economic success. Since the first PLAYMOBIL man was made, geobra Brandstätter has invested approximately 300 million Euros in moulds alone. The injection moulding machine melts the granulated plastic and injects it into the moulds under high pressure. The finished PLAYMOBIL part falls out of the machine at the bottom—or, in the case of large parts, such as the hull of Noah's ark, it is lifted out by robot arms. A machine can produce a ship's hull in 30 seconds. Once the machines have been programmed, everything runs automatically until the predetermined quota has been reached. Where tricky parts are concerned—such as the doors of the RCE train, which are moulded with the window in place—each door is checked individually. After all, quality is the greatest commandment at PLAYMOBIL. The PLAYMOBIL moulding plant operates around the clock in three shifts. Approximately four million individual parts are cast every day; about 80 million per month. All of the plastic sprue that falls out of the injection machines is ground up again and processed into new PLAYMOBIL parts.

PLASTIC

PLAYMOBIL toys are up to 95 percent plastic, primarily ABS (acrylonitrile-butadiene-styrene copolymers), but also polystyrene, polyamide, polyethylene and similar materials. It goes without saying that PLAYMOBIL toys are PVC free. The company uses only high-quality materials that meet all standards of quality, stability, safety, colouring, function and hygiene. The plastic is neutral and does not emit any toxins; it is resistant to saliva and perspiration. The only thing you shouldn't do is leave your PLAYMOBIL family out in the sun for days at a time: Despite their UV filter, the colours will eventually fade.

Behind closed doors

The PLAYMOBIL pieces are printed using a so-called tampon printing technique. Here, the airliner wings get their stripes and positioning lights, and the police department gets its sign. The machines can print up to ten different colours—a relief for parents, who used to have to apply the stickers included in the packages as exactly as possible. In addition, today's printing is much more permanent.

Behind closed doors

Left: PLAYMOBIL figures are made up of seven basic pieces: two arms, a head with wig, torso with inner mechanism and leg element. If assembled in the proper order, they simply require a firm pressing on the head, and everything snaps into place.

Right: The chimpanzees emerge from the machine completely mobile and fully assembled.

HOW THE CONTROL COLUMN GETS INTO THE AIRLINER

Once all the individual parts have been cast, they are then printed and assembled. Even though many parents still groan over the tedious detail work they have to perform once they have unpacked the twelve plastic bags of the knights' castle,—they have no idea how much of the work has already been done for them. Let's take, for example, the chimpanzees that swing around in the zoo and on Noah's ark. For technical reasons, they drop out of the moulding machine with their heads turned backwards, so that the contact point of the moulding frame will be on the back of the head and not in the middle of the face. So now each chimpanzee's head needs to be turned back around—a laborious job, which has also been passed on to correctional facilities. Other tasks, like the pre-assembly of the jet airliner, are performed directly in Dietenhofen. Here, efficient "aeroplane builders" click the rows of seats and the control column into the body of the plane. Directly adjacent to them is the tampon printing machine, which adds the jaunty stripes and the red and green position lights onto the wings. The machine can apply up to ten colours simultaneously—thus, parents and children have long been spared having to accurately stick on license plates or police badges.

The smaller parts which are not pre-assembled are placed in so-called preliminary bags according to an intricately devised plan. The employees at the factory—or the at-home workers in their garages—sit at a large sorting table and place three flower boxes, 20 flowers, a mailbox, a mailbox cover and three outdoor lamps into each polyethylene bag. This is then sealed with the push of a pedal and drops onto a scale. Only when its weight is exactly right—meaning there is not one piece too many or too few—does it land in the box. Preliminary bags, aeroplane halves, pieces of walls, and many other items are initially stored in the high rack warehouse until, based on the production plan, it is their turn to be packed.

The PLAYMOBIL figures, which—with the exception of the babies—are all manufactured on Malta, also wait here before finally taking their places in the blue boxes.

Behind closed doors

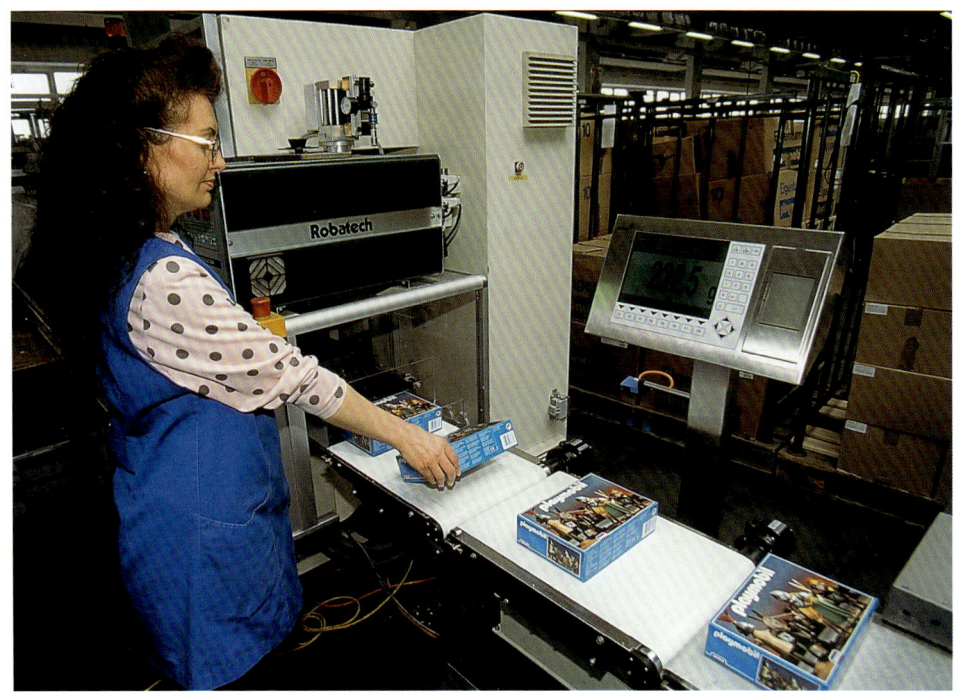

The weight has to be correct down to the last gram: This means that the package has been assembled properly, with no part too many or too few. The boxes are stored on pallets in the high rack warehouse, which—at 459 feet long, 164 feet wide and 98 feet high—can only be organised by a computer. It alone knows where to find a pirate ship or a police station. As a precaution, the warehouse is also equipped with an emergency backup generator, so that delivery need not stop in case of a power outage. Trucks carry the blue boxes from the 15 loading ramps out into the big, wide world.

DOWN TO THE LAST GRAM—7227 GRAMS OF CASTLE

On long packing lines, many hands fill the PLAYMOBIL packages with preliminary bags and individual parts. The process starts with the bottom half of the box being opened up. The box then travels along the conveyor belt, past up to ten employees, until every part that belongs in the new zoo or knights' castle is actually in the package. Along the way, the contents are repeatedly weighed; deviations may not exceed three grams. Packages which are too heavy or too light are sorted out and must be checked by hand. At the end, a brochure is added, the assembly instructions are inserted, and the lid is put on. Adhesive seals protect the package from pre-sale plundering. Finally, the 50 knights' castles or 100 zoos are stacked onto a pallet, which makes its way back to the high rack warehouse to await shipment to international markets. The high rack warehouse was put into operation in 1979; in 1990, its capacity was doubled. 28,000 pallets are stored in a space 367 feet long, 98 feet high and 164 feet wide. Approximately 30 million Euros worth of PLAYMOBIL is stored here. The entire warehouse operates automatically, and out of the multitude of products, only a computer can locate exactly the item that is needed at any given time. To protect against a possible power loss, the warehouse has its own emergency backup generator.

Behind closed doors

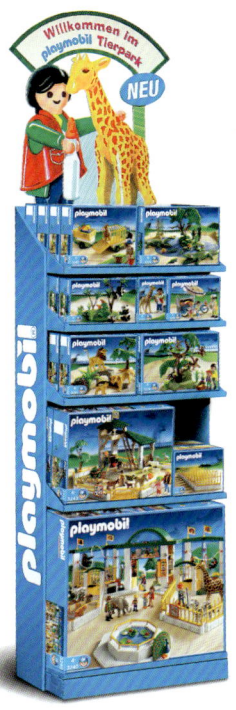

WELL PLACED ON CARDBOARD SHELVES

In keeping with PLAYMOBIL custom, new products are always presented in the stores in special display cases. Thus, for example, the zoo series appeared on a blue cardboard shelf with a large baby giraffe display. All the packages belonging to that play world could be found there—the pandas, the lion family, the monkeys with their climbing tree, the alligators, the ice cream man, the baby giraffe, and, of course, the large zoo package. These and any other new product packages which have been ordered since the Toy Fair travel by truck from Dietenhofen to the toy shops, warehouses or department stores promptly in time for the sales launch. Repeat orders are handled differently. So-called commissioners assemble orders daily in the high rack warehouse. Using electric vehicles, they jet along three special aisles of the warehouse in which all the PLAYMOBIL articles are stacked; they collect the packages which have been ordered and bring them to the shipping department.

In the order picking area, all items that are available for delivery can be found individually. Here, workers assemble the orders which arrive daily from toy dealerships.

THE ENVIRONMENT—WASTE REDUCTION—RECYCLING

Trash has been an issue at PLAYMOBIL since the very beginning. The "garbage men" have been in the mix since 1978, and the big PLAYMOBIL men and women also make an effort to produce as little garbage as possible. Plastic waste is almost non-existent, since plastic sprue and any defective products are ground up again and flow back into the production process. Mixed materials which cannot be reused for making PLAYMOBIL pieces are passed on to a specialised firm which manufactures recycled products such as garden fences, benches and flower boxes.

Of course, PLAYMOBIL also uses tons of paper. Whenever possible, the company uses recycled paper—for example, in the transport packaging, which is made of corrugated cardboard with a high percentage of recycled material. Even more packaging is saved in the transport of materials from the suppliers to the headquarters in Dietenhofen: Here, reusable packaging has been in use for some time.

The so-called shrink-wrap which was used as an outer seal for the larger boxes has also long since disappeared from shop counters. In the past, this was used to improve the appearance of the packages as well as to protect small parts from being stolen. Nowadays, locking flaps and adhesive seals guard against potential pilferers instead. The blue boxes themselves have a recycled paper content of 80 to 95 percent, and thanks to the special inks used for printing, they can also be reprocessed. The little plastic bags inside the packages are unavoidable, but they are made of low-pressure polyethylene which doesn't damage the groundwater in landfills and is completely non-toxic when burnt.

The waste heat from the injection moulding machines is converted into heat energy. Not only is this process kinder to the environment, but it reduces heating oil usage at the Dietenhofen plant by half. But above all, the product itself contributes to waste reduction, since almost nothing gets thrown away. Rather, when children grow too old to play with the toys, they are passed on to relatives, sold, collected or auctioned off on the Internet.

10,000 REPLACEMENT PARTS AT THE TOUCH OF A BUTTON

Vacuum cleaners and sandboxes are the natural enemies of PLAYMOBIL, since tiny parts can disappear here never to be seen again. Admittedly, extremely lightweight parts are sometimes missing from the very beginning, since their absence may not show up on the weight check. So what do you do if the knight's sword disappears in the outwork pipe, the firefighter is missing his white cuffs or your careless grandmother steps on the hay wagon? No problem: Every replacement part is still available at geobra Brandstätter for five years. A multitude of orders for replacement parts arrive in Dietenhofen every day—whether by telephone, by post or e-mail. Here, six paternoster lifts are filed to the brim with little boxes, waiting to

Behind closed doors

make sad children happy again or to realise the creative wishes of builders or collectors. For some time now, the orders that come in do not just request new axles, lost police antennas or additional chicks; there are lists which ask for ten sets of shelves or 20 folding chairs as well.

Each individual part that exists at PLAYMOBIL has its own numerical code. When this is entered into the computer, just the right drawer in the right paternoster will be quickly located.

Of course, there are also replacements available for torn box lids—requested primarily by toy dealers—or for new assembly instructions, if the old ones are missing. Directly adjacent in the warehouse, the little plastic bags for direct service are stacked. The service department has been in existence since 1983—a beneficial facility for anyone who is simply looking for a few replacement parts, a single little building or accessory, without having to buy another giant package. At first, toy shops did not react positively to the direct service department: Dealers were afraid that geobra Brandstätter wanted to take over part of the business themselves. But it soon became clear that direct service is just another step toward customer loyalty. After all, almost no other toy manufacturer offers the level of service that PLAYMOBIL does. And satisfied customers are always happy to buy more...

"Unfortunately, while unpacking the product, I noticed that the contents did not match the contents specification on the box. Two shields were missing. Since my son is a very enthusiastic PLAYMOBIL player and would have loved to have the two shields, could you please see whether it is possible to send them to me?" Bärbel R., Hamburg, 1975

"My request: Please send me (C.O.D. to my address), two generous handfuls of tools (including mortar trough); a few workers' hats and vests; knights' weapons and a few helmets; and especially Indian weapons and tools, including head-dresses and collars." Andreas S., certified engineer, Augsburg, 1975

Amid the typical PLAYMOBIL chaos in the playroom, a few small pieces tend to get lost. The service department offers replacement parts for many years.

Behind closed doors

A decision is made as to what the display should look like; then the police scene goes into mass production—in this case, in Dutch blue, since the police officers for the international market wear blue uniforms with English lettering. Only the robbers look the same everywhere.

The display scenes are stabilised with a hot glue gun. Shops have the option of buying or leasing them—a service which has been available since the very beginning.

PLAYMOBIL'S PLAYROOM IS CALLED THE DISPLAY DEPARTMENT

The display department produces over 1000 miniature worlds every year. Countless parts are stored in handy plastic slipcovers, making the heart of every PLAYMOBIL fan beat faster. But in case anyone would want to apply for her job immediately, the woman with the hot glue gun dampens the enthusiasm somewhat: "When you're assembling the 100th farm scene, it quickly becomes monotonous. No, I don't have to look at the assembly instructions anymore—except maybe if I've been on holiday for three weeks," she explains, clicking the proper roof panel onto the proper end of a building with the ease of a sleepwalker. But the piece-work decorators allow themselves a little creative freedom as well: "We sometimes incorporate a little joke; we break off a rung from the ladder or bend the front wheel of a bicycle so that it couldn't actually drive anymore."

The display department is as old as PLAYMOBIL itself. At the time of the very first presentation, Hans Beck spent the night shift building platforms and display construction sites in order to properly show the little men in action. In-house, the department has long been known as "castle-building", since the castle walls and battlements are built here for the knights out of Styrofoam and cardboard before they receive their own PLAYMOBIL castle.

Behind closed doors

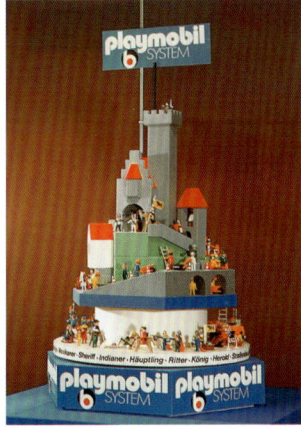

From the first Styrofoam castles—which have to serve for the PLAYMOBIL knights until they receive their own plastic ones—to realistic display window decorations, there is nothing the display department can't do.
The remote controlled "Playmo-X" is a copy of the Robot (item 3591) from the space series. It appeared for the first time at the 1984 Toy Fair in Nuremberg and was so well-received that it was loaned out to various toy shops afterwards.

Toy dealerships can choose to buy or lease the display pieces and sets. They come in various sizes and may be rotating or equipped with lighting. During the Christmas season—which begins earlier every year—you can press your nose flat on display cases and shop windows and write a complete wish list. The displays are available in different sizes and price classes—for example, simply an assembled zoo package (item 3240) or a 3-by-6 foot large display scene decorated with every item included in the series. Large department stores such as Kaufhof's Kidzz World in the Oberhausen CentrO set up display cases containing all of the current play worlds, as

Behind closed doors

Elaborate window displays kick off the Christmas shopping season.

Behind closed doors

The large contest figure, which is filled to the brim with little PLAYMOBIL figures, receives an excellent response in major department stores.

For the Tour of Germany bicycle race, which passed through Dietenhofen in 2003, the display department built a matching model for the television broadcast. The road was movable, and the spectators remained stationary along the sides, creating the impression that the cyclists were actually speeding past.

well as an extra play table where customers can try out the products. For exhibits such as these, the decorators will even stray from the PLAYMOBIL scale and build extra-large cranes, six-foot-high Nessies that have glowing eyes and can spit smoke or cars which you could almost drive.

The "playroom" also makes the life-sized PLAYMOBIL figures who point the way in display windows or at shop entrances. There are versions for indoor use as well as weather-proof figures for outdoors—for example, for the FunPark. The most recently-added display piece is the contest figure, which is filled to the brim with little Playmos and displayed in large toy departments. If you correctly guess how many figures are inside, you could win a big prize drawing.

Special orders, such as the design of a railroad display for New York's largest toy store, FAO Schwartz on Fifth Avenue, are naturally an extra treat. But the decorators also found a perfect solution for building a miniature copy of the Tour of Germany bicycle race. When one leg of the race passed by the PLAYMOBIL factory in Dietenhofen in the spring of 2003, TV stations cleverly inter-cut the PLAYMOBIL scene with footage from the actual race.

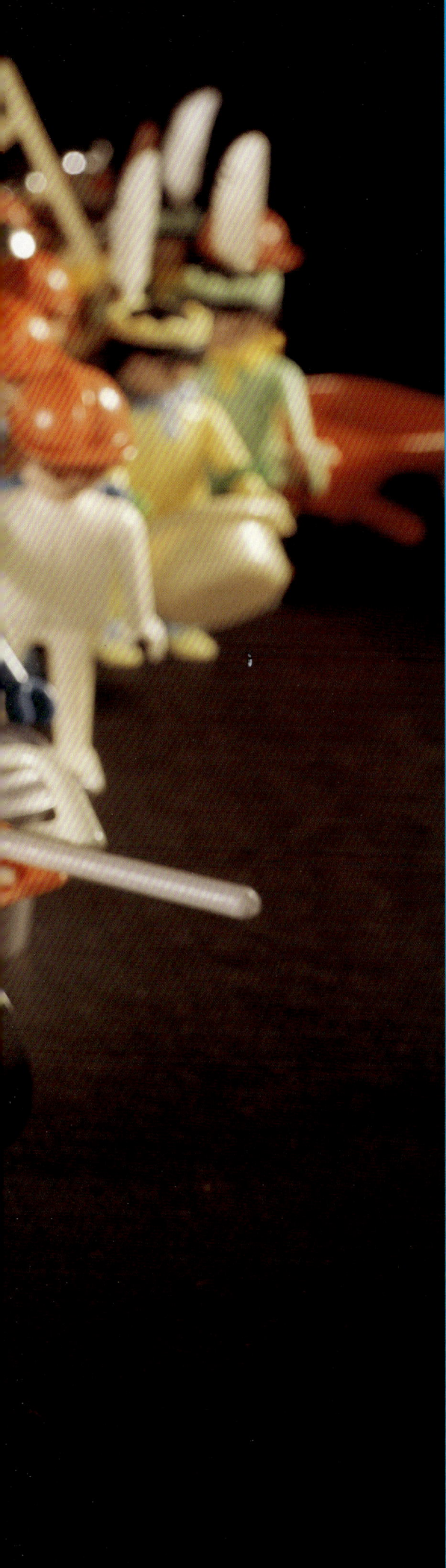

PLAYMOBIL— a timeline

Over 30 years of PLAYMOBIL—that is, of the peaceful occupation of the playroom, a toy idea "Made in Germany" which has expanded to include the entire world. That means over 30 years of new developments, international awards, the German Federal Cross of Merit for the company chief, a bust of Hans Beck at the Expo, and playtime fun a billion times over. But it also means enormous investments, entrepreneurial courage, a years-long battle against would-be imitators and the consolidation of the geobra Brandstätter GmbH toy empire.

from the beginnings to the present day

 1974

February 2, 1974: The PLAYMOBIL System makes its first official appearance at the company trade fair at geobra Brandstätter in Zirndorf, which is held in parallel to the Nuremberg Toy Fair. The product series introduced are examples of the three types of play worlds that PLAYMOBIL still differentiates today:
1. History, represented by the knights;
2. Other cultures, in this case, Indians; and
3. Contemporary themes: The first representatives of this area are the construction workers. Quite realistically, the Construction Accessories set (item 3112) consists of a wheelbarrow, a hand roller, ten traffic cones, three beer crates and 18 beer bottles. In the next catalogue, the PLAYMOBIL men express their thanks with the following dialogue:
Yellow worker: "This is already my fifth bottle today."
Green worker: "No problem. There's plenty of beer here."
The Youth Ministry, however, is quick to object.

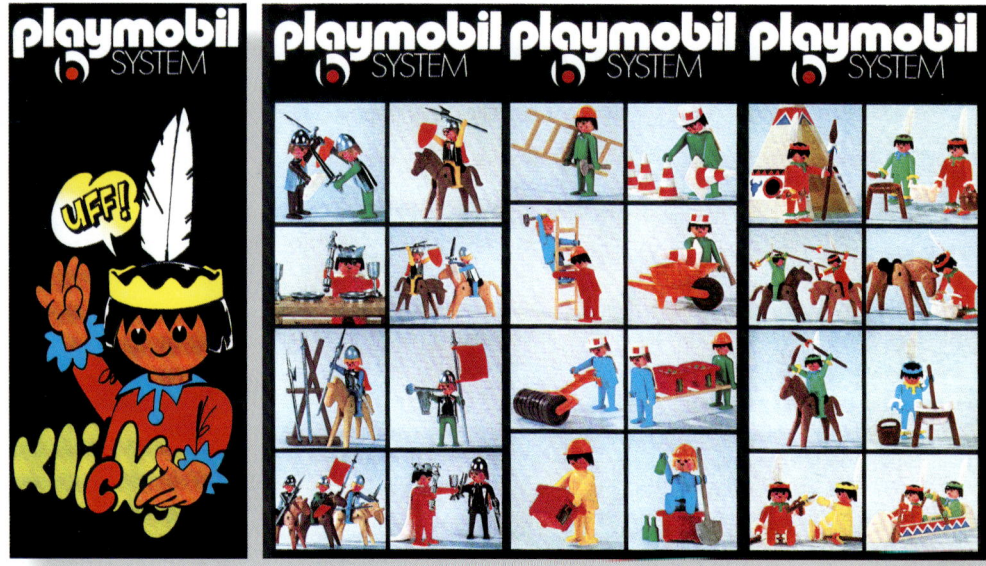

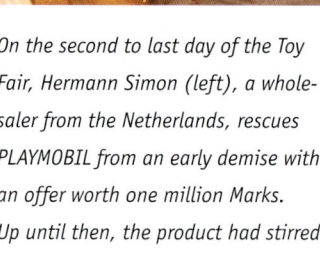

On the second to last day of the Toy Fair, Hermann Simon (left), a wholesaler from the Netherlands, rescues PLAYMOBIL from an early demise with an offer worth one million Marks. Up until then, the product had stirred little interest.

from the beginnings to the present day

1975

New to the assortment: The first international police officer—still in blue and white with a police inscription on his helmet—cowboys, Yankee soldiers and travellers. PLAYMOBIL receives the "Spiel gut" seal of approval, and in the Netherlands, it is awarded the coveted "Toy of the Year" trophy for the first time.

The slightly different little men from the BIG toy factory arrive on the market. An ex-geobra employee is rumoured to have passed on the idea. The PlayBIG figures are four inches high with legs and feet which move independently. Initially, BIG copies PLAYMOBIL's ideas completely and introduces construction workers, knights and Indians onto the market. These are followed later by heavily armed soldiers and Vikings. Opinions in the trade are divided as to which system is the better one; however, due to the difference in size, they are not very compatible with each other. Brandstätter and BIG head Bettag fight a "little man war" in the courts over market shares and whether or not PlayBIG is a copyright infringement.

"Each of us is spending about 50,000 Marks a month on attorney and court costs," estimates Brandstätter. His company wins in the first and second hearings. Bettag appeals, and the courts finally rule that his figures are individual products. In the meantime, three years have gone by, and the market has made its own decision.

The PlayBIG figures are not popular with children. Production stops in the 1978–79 season; the remaining products are still sold for a few more years. The BIG company achieves worldwide fame with its Bobbycar, and the fight between the two companies becomes ancient history...

75

from the beginnings to the present day

a police van and lots of police officers (now in West German green as well), an operating room and hospital nurses with wheelchairs and firefighters with a hook-and-ladder truck. The cowboys get the first buildings, in the form of a bank, a hotel, a saloon, a sheriff's office, a drugstore and a stable. The Yankee soldiers can retreat into their fort and are given the first cannon to defend themselves.

Beginning this year, the noble knights can duel for the favours of a beautiful damsel. A large dowry chest awaits the winner. Since so much PLAYMOBIL is now flying off to so many different countries, Lufthansa Airlines is pleased as well and presents the boss with its highest award—a V.I.P. pin. The family firm of geobra Brandstätter celebrates its 100th anniversary, and Horst Brandstätter pulls out all the stops. The trade magazine Spielzeug Markt lists the menu in detail: "Goose liver pâté with quail eggs, lingonberries, toast; consommé, Dalmatian-style scampi, steak with porcini mushrooms, cauliflower, spinach and mimosa salad; assorted cheeses; flambéed strawberries with vanilla ice cream"—and reports that "the successful festivities continued into the early morning hours".

Horst Brandstätter with one of the first framework houses.

 1976

One year after the UN proclaims the Year of the Woman, PLAYMOBIL brings its first female figures onto the market. They are easily recognisable with flippy miniskirts and medium-length hair—although still lacking breasts, which will not appear until 13 years later.

The PLAYMOBIL assortment is expanded to reflect the turbulence of daily life: There is

1977

The knights of the PLAYMOBIL order increase their supremacy. With the first knights' castle and numerous houses—including a blacksmith's shop, a bakery and an inn—medieval city life is reborn in long-lasting plastic. A very contemporary contrast is the vehicle series, which conjures up five different models from one basic form: the family car, police car, ADAC (emergency auto service) car, emergency doctor and fire chief's cars. And where previously there were only travellers, there are now travel vehicles, in the form of a camper and a mobile home. Apparently, all of these can drive as far as the North Pole, since there is no other explanation for the sudden appearance of a polar bear family. In the same year, the English toy industry is so impressed by PLAYMOBIL that they name it "Toy of the Year" in that country. And in the first "Zirndorf Sweepstakes"—which have since become famous both for prizes and number of participants—a lucky winner is awarded his or her weight in PLAYMOBIL.

from the beginnings to the present day

With Horst Brandstätter and "King PLAYMOBIL" standing by, the winner of the 1977 sweepstakes is awarded his weight in PLAYMOBIL.

Der Herbst '77 bringt den größten Hit, seit es PLAYMOBIL gibt. Nicht nur eine Burg – eine ganze Stadt läßt PLAYMOBIL wachsen. Historisch, aber ebenso gegenwartsbezogen. Nahezu unbegrenzte Spielmöglichkeiten durch viele Variationen und liebevolle Details faszinieren nicht nur die Kinder und bringen Spitzenumsätze für den Handel. Jedes Gebäude kann einzeln gekauft werden. Neben der PLAYMOBIL-Stadt sind ab Herbst '77 weitere PLAYMOBIL-Neuheiten, wie Flugzeug, Hubschrauber oder Traktor, lieferbar.

from the beginnings to the present day

1978

With 56 new product packages, PLAYMOBIL sets to work populating the entire country. To facilitate the push into new territories, as of this year, the little people can also travel by air (in a two-seater propeller aeroplane and a helicopter) and by water. Along with a small excursion boat, in 1978, PLAYMOBIL launches the pirate ship. It hits the market like a broadside, and within six months, approximately 100,000 pirate ships have conquered German bathtubs and playrooms. Two years later, the buccaneer fleet has grown to half a million worldwide, and the 500,000th ship sails into the Nuremberg toy museum in 1980. Incidentally, one of the pirates is a native of the Caribbean, and with him, the first black PLAYMOBIL people enter the assortment.

The "PLAYMOBIL Colour" series, introduced at Eastertime, brings even more colour and imagination along with it. Using waterproof, permanent felt-tip markers, every child can become his or her own designer. In a nationwide colouring contest, Hans Beck and Horst Brandstätter are nearly at their wits' end in trying to select a first-prize winner among the 58,000 entries they receive. In addition, the circus comes to PLAYMOBIL Land, inspiring expansion ideas for many years to come.

On 25 November 1978, the film The Playmos are Coming has its premiere at the Nuremberg Rex-Kino cinema. The peaceful invasion of the earth by the little figures from Planet Omega is 30 minutes long. The entertaining film is subsequently screened in a decommissioned double-decker Berlin city bus, which is decorated with PLAYMOBIL motifs. It tours through Germany, Austria, France and Switzerland carrying lots of PLAYMOBIL Colour, with the aim of bringing the play idea to the people.

from the beginnings to the present day

The film The Playmos are Coming arrives on the market first,
followed by an appropriate TV camera team from PLAYMOBIL.

from the beginnings to the present day

 **1979**

In light of all this success, it is high time to put a high rack warehouse into operation in Dietenhofen. Its impressive proportions are 367 feet long by 98 feet high and 95 feet wide. If we consider that a PLAMOBIL figure is just 2.9 inches high...
Construction of the warehouse costs 11 million Marks, but after all—it can hold 12,000 pallets containing products worth a total of over 70 million Marks.
The colour idea has sold well, and the company expands on it with such products as the "PLAYMOBIL Play Boxes"—packages containing two colouring figures and a 20-page play newspaper.

A shovel excavator, a farm and a television broadcast van are introduced for the first time. The circus theme is expanded.

In connection with the International Year of the Child, geobra advertises a PLAYMOBIL city competition, calling upon cities and communities to do more for children. Thirty-five communities participate and document the improvements they make in day-to-day living conditions for children. The national committee for the Year of the Child takes over the judging process, and the towns of Habichtswald, Herrieden and Fürth are declared the winners. Each community receives 7,000 Marks in cash from geobra, plus 3,000 Marks' worth of PLAYMOBIL toys.

Since the plastic injection moulding plant is growing, and new moulds have to be manufactured every year at an annual cost of several million Marks, geobra begins training its own plastic mould makers. In 1979, the first three trainees complete their course with top marks.

Five years after PLAYMOBIL's introduction onto the market, its name recognition rating is 67 percent, according to a study by the GfK (Gesellschaft für Konsumforschung—consumer research institute). Nine years later, 87 percent of respondents recognise the brand name; today, the rate is nearly 100 percent.

from the beginnings to the present day

1980

PLAYMOBIL receives the "Brunte"—the Swedish toy "Oscar"—for the best toy in that country. By now, 320 million PLAYMOBIL figures populate the whole world. No wonder, then, that they also want to venture into space. Initially, the series only appears in the catalogue: Manufacturing does not actually start until 1981, since the production and distribution departments are already working at full capacity on the rest of the assortment. After all, 1980 is supposed to be PLAYMOBIL's most successful year yet.

A population of this size can no longer do without a railroad, either. The first electric PLAYMOBIL train—with a track gauge of 1, corresponding to the scale of 1:24—runs on tracks made by the E.P. Lehmann company (known for its LGB garden railroad). It is a toy train, not a model train, PLAYMOBIL emphasises—since the target group is child and father, and not father and child.

In this and in the following year, several Bavarian and Westphalian savings bank branches hold colouring contests using the PLAYMOBIL Colour figures. Each branch registers between 300 and 400 children for the competition. The prize is—what else?—PLAYMOBIL. But nobody goes home empty-handed, since each child can reclaim his or her coloured figure from the branch at the end of the competition.

Four weeks before Christmas, PLAYMOBIL is awarded the entire main display window at FAO Schwartz on Fifth Avenue in New York—the most famous toy store in the world. For the 6 1/2 by 16-foot display window, workers in Zirndorf manufacture and assemble three winter-themed PLAYMOBIL railroad display pieces with a diameter of 55 inches each—and immediately take them apart again to be packed in a ship's container.

In New York, the FAO Schwartz decorators rebuild the winter dream with the help of pictures and instructions from Zirndorf and give PLAYMOBIL's business an enormous boost. In Germany, PLAYMOBIL establishes its own field service to directly support its sales partners.

from the beginnings to the present

 1981

The Fachverband Konsum-Kunststoffwaren (consumer plastic products association) in Frankfurt names PLAYMOBIL its "Product of the Year" for 1981, and the design-center in Stuttgart chooses it for its "1981 German Selection", which presents an annual overview of the best designs in German industrial products.
In September, offspring finally arrive in the PLAYMOBIL family. In response to numerous requests and queries from fans large and small, child figures appear on the market. The girls and boys are 0.78 inches smaller than their parents are, but the inner surface area of their hands is identical, allowing them to hold onto any accessory piece. Furthermore, they are the first figures with rotating wrists, a development in which the full-sized figures no longer want to lag behind. In toy stores, the new figures are sold—using the not-so-original slogan, "Hey kids, now there are PLAYMOBIL kids!"—in four packages: "Children's Playroom", "Playground", "Children with Vehicles" and "Mother with Child". Sales are excellent: so good that at 28 million Marks, the invoice value of the October profits is nearly as high as the company's entire annual revenue for 1971. Since the French have been enthusiastic PLAYMOBIL customers from the very beginning, the founding of PLAYMOBIL France in 1981 marks the launch of the firm's most important distribution subsidiary. The company headquarters is in Evry-Cedex, outside of Paris. England, too, has had its own subsidiary company since 1980—PLAYMOBIL (UK) Ltd. in Swansea.

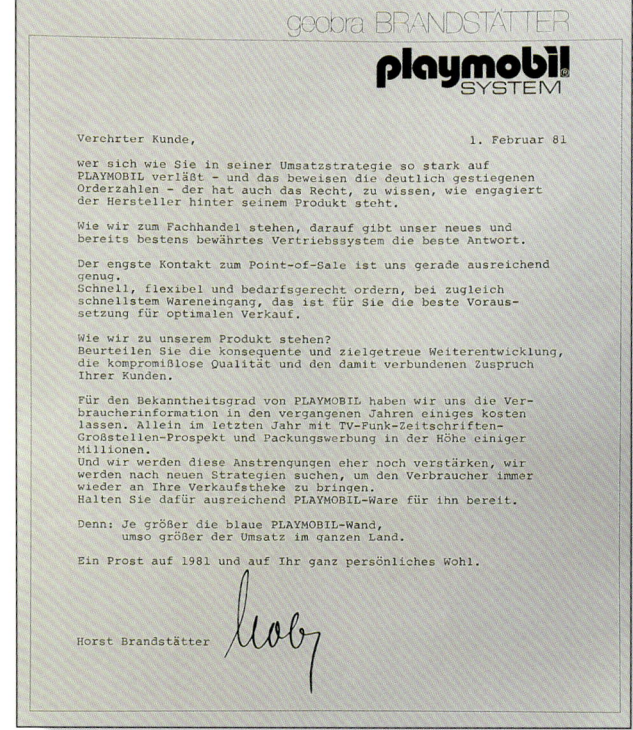

In a letter to distributors at the beginning of 1981, Horst Brandstätter assures his sales partners that geobra will continue its intensive advertising efforts and urges them to help maximise profits by keeping PLAYMOBIL prominently displayed on their shelves.

 1982

The adult PLAYMOBIL figures are now given movable, flesh-coloured hands as well. On Malta, Brand International Ltd. is awarded the "Phoenicia Trade Trophy", the Maltese government's business prize for excellent export results.
In 1982, the Fachverband Konsum-Kunststoffwaren presents an award to the hook-and-ladder fire truck; in 1983, the Pottery Shop is honoured.
PLAYMOBIL Japan is founded and attempts to compete with the popularity of family computers on the Japanese market. In order to whet Japanese children's appetites for PLAYMOBIL, the company undertakes a cooperative venture with the Japanese biscuit company, Meiji. Each package of cookies contains a PLAYMOBIL figure—a move that helps spread the product across the country.

The Direct Service Catalogue, containing supplementary and replacement parts, appears for the first time. Here, you can also find some of the products which have been removed from the assortment. In all other cases as well, the PLAYMOBIL customer service department processes every replacement request for lost or defective parts quickly and conscientiously.

The Space Rover appears as a supplement to the Space Station.

from the beginnings to the present day

 1983

"Spiel gut" awards rain down one after the other—for the Overhead Crane, the First Aid Station, Ngorongoro Station, the Farm Tractor and Shed, the Farm House set and the Freight Terminal. And in a test of electric toy trains, the Stiftung Warentest (product testing foundation) gives the PLAYMOBIL train its highest rating, "very good".

The Glow-in-the-Dark Ghost (item 3317) comes on the market and quickly becomes a bestseller. By the end of the year, 320,000 ghosts are haunting children's rooms. Naturally, the secret of its luminosity has worried parents up in arms, suspecting unhealthy contents. But Brandstätter has had the figure tested by the LGA (a product safety testing organisation), which certifies that no radioactive materials were used.

The PLAYMOBIL figures are ageing, and the first grandparents appear—easily recognisable with their white hair and beards for the grandpas. And the teacher from the "Teacher and Class" package (item 3560) becomes the first PLAYMOBIL figure to wear glasses.

At the Broadcasting Exhibition in Berlin, the Saba company uses a giant PLAYMOBIL city, complete with railroad, as an attractive backdrop for amateur filmmakers trying out its new video cameras.

1984

PLAYMOBIL Land turns ten years old; its population has grown to 500 million little people. Submitting fantasy-filled pictures and stories, 22,500 children take part in the drawing and writing contest, "Imagination Wins". Since a total of only 1,500

prizes can be awarded, each participant receives a PLAYMOBIL key chain as a consolation prize.

Once again, there is a new addition to the family: The PLAYMOBIL baby is a bouncing 1.4 inches long at birth. The most special thing about him is that he comes out of the moulding machine completely finished, with movable arms and a rotating head, injected with three different colours of plastic. This was a technological first at the time—just like the fully jointed chimpanzee.

At the Nuremberg Toy Fair, the "Playmo-X" robot delights visitors and is later loaned out to toy shops around the country. It is a "life size" version of the little Robot (item 3591) from the space series, which—not coincidentally—looks a lot like R2D2 from Star Wars.

For the first time, the 1984–85 PLAYMOBIL catalogue appears with large photographs and a wish list on the back cover.

from the beginnings to the present day

1985

At the Didacta Education Trade Fair in Stuttgart, PLAYMOBIL introduces a series especially for kindergartens, which consists primarily of animals, figures with small vehicles, construction vehicles, a playground, police, go-carts and zoo accessories.
And at the International Model Train Exhibition in Frankfurt, a little steam train chugs through the "Fantasy Playland". Every item that the PLAYMOBIL play worlds have to offer is set up over a space of 6,000 sq. ft. The net proceeds from the train tickets go to the charity "Aktion Sorgenkind".
By now, the PLAYMOBIL people have ventured as far as the Arctic, where they meet their Eskimo relatives, complete with igloo, dog sled and kayak.
Mattel, the Barbie company, now markets PLAYMOBIL in the USA and Canada, but the hoped-for success is not achieved, and the cooperation ends after a relatively short time.
As in the previous year, a Christmas brochure is released, containing 20 pages

85

from the beginnings to the present day

of nice, child-friendly PLAYMOBIL stories. It is inserted in relevant general-interest and parents' magazines such as Stern, Eltern or Bussi-Bär. Not surprisingly, the story focuses on the Christmas sales theme for that year, providing suggestions for the wish list. From March through December, filling up your tank at an Esso service station in Canada is a doubly good deal. Once your point card has been "filled up" with at least 150 litres of fuel, you can receive the 160-piece PLAYMOBIL Esso service station at one-fourth of the normal price, or one of five other packages. If Canada is too far away, German customers can purchase the Esso station using the item number 3434. The PLAYMOBIL passenger train with steam locomotive is among the top ten wished for items for Christmas 1985.

 1986

In the winter of 1985–86, 130,000 children take part in the Christmas sweepstakes. The assignment is to find an Eskimo boy who is hidden in the catalogue in nine different places.
A subsidiary distribution company is founded in the Netherlands.
After ten years of sluggish business, geobra has had enough, and establishes its own distribution subsidiaries overseas. PLAYMOBIL USA Inc. is based in Edison, New Jersey. PLAYMOBIL Canada Inc. has its headquarters in Mississauga, near Toronto. Each company offers 100 items, some of them Americanised. In the USA, for example, the little cannons on the pirate ship are not allowed to shoot for safety reasons.
After twelve prosperous years, a few of the PLAYMOBIL men—the clown, for example—have gained a little belly.

1987

The PLAYMOBIL women are given breasts and long skirts, which frustrate some children, since they no longer fit on the horses. Fortunately, the new Western railroad is steaming through the Old West city, so they can ride on this instead.

The rescue helicopter receives the "Toy of the Year" award in the Netherlands.

The cost for the helicopter moulds alone (27 new moulds have been manufactured) is close to one million Marks.

Audio cassettes are introduced onto the market in cooperation with EUROPA, with Hansjörg Felmy as the narrator. With the help of a magical piece of wood containing the ghosts of Indian medicine men, Professor Mobilux and his Irish assistant, Patrick F. Patrick, are able to travel through time and space as they choose. Naturally, they only travel to the sorts of scenarios which can be re-enacted with currently-available PLAYMOBIL products: For example, they travel on the new Western Railroad to Silver Ranch. The appropriate figures are available as a set with the item number 3099.

Professor Mobilux and Patrick F. Patrick are the main characters in a series of story cassettes.

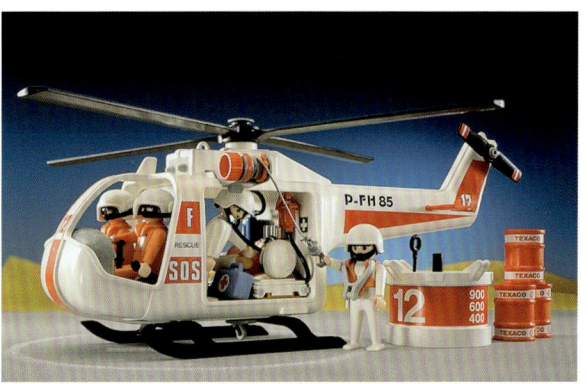

from the beginnings to the present day

In 1988, the first zoo opens in PLAYMOBIL Land, containing many exotic animals.

from the beginnings to the present day

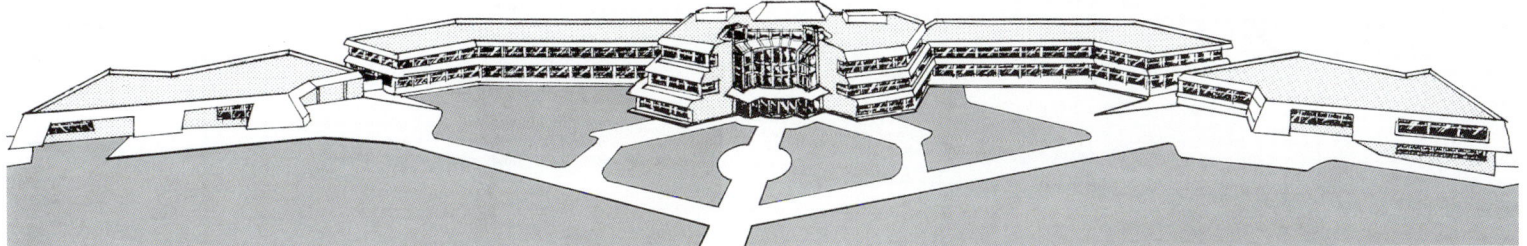

 1988

In early February, the cornerstone is laid for the new, futuristic-looking administration building in Zirndorf.

In Germany, the rescue helicopter is awarded the "Spiel gut" seal and is named "Product of the Year 1988" by the Fachverband Konsum-Kunststoffwaren.

The first complete PLAYMOBIL zoo comes onto the market. And with new pigmentation, the Indians finally become true "redskins".

Two 20-page booklets with child-friendly illustrations are inserted into major magazines during the pre-Christmas season: The Endless Journey, the story of a little ghost; and for smaller children, Beppo—A Clown Looking for a Circus.

The Brandstätter Development Association for Innovation, Market Research, Design, Model Building, Quality Control and Product and Mould Construction is founded. Under the direction of Hans Beck, around 50 specialists now work constantly to develop new PLAYMOBIL ideas.

 1989

Up to now, three-quarters of all "true" PLAYMOBIL fans have been boys. The nostalgic 1900 series is the first group of products that primarily targets girls ages six years and older. The packaging for this series is not blue, but pink.

"The Good Old Days" is the advertising slogan for the new product line. PLAYMOBIL collectors are impressed as well. Four hundred new injection moulding tools are required to produce the new series, at a cost of ten million Marks.

In Canada, the entire PLAYMOBIL product line is named "Toy of the Year".

from the beginnings to the present day

 1990

PLAYMOBIL 2-4, the product line for toddlers, makes its debut and is soon renamed PLAYMOBIL 1.2.3, since it is actually appropriate for children aged $1^1/_2$ years and up. Early introduction to the brand and customer loyalty are important.
The second version of the pirate ship, with new rigging, conquers the oceans of the world. Now on board are a red-bearded captain, a Chinese cook, a female pirate and a ship's boy. For the first time, we see barefoot figures, figures with boots and a pirate with a wooden leg.
The PLAYMOBIL FunPark opens in Zirndorf. Its still-small dimensions include a display area, PLAYMOBIL play spaces, a parts and pick-up warehouse, a hospitality centre and a miniature company museum.
Due to the development of PLAYMOBIL 1.2.3 and the 1900 line, there are fewer other new products in the main "blue series".

from the beginnings to the present day

 1991

Field service employees are provided with Toshiba laptop computers. The program they use was developed at geobra: Salespeople can record dealers' orders via bar code; the data are transmitted to Zirndorf through the German postal service's DATEX-P network the same evening.

For the first time, PLAYMOBIL's advertising budget rises to the double digits in millions of Marks.

Once again, someone else attempts to take a slice out of PLAYMOBIL's profits: Carrera introduces its "play o.k." figures, including an automobile workshop, a fire station, a roadway repair service and a pond with fishermen. PLAYMOBIL responds with a lawsuit, but a final verdict will not be reached until 1994.

June 1: In honour of "Children's Day", the PLAYMOBIL FunPark makes its official debut with an open house celebration, attended

Horst Brandstätter joins Fürth's District Administrator—the Children's Day patron—and young visitors in colouring giant white figures with fingerpaints.

by approximately 8,000 guests. (The Day of the Child, celebrated on the first weekend in June, corresponds to International Children's Day, which, before German reunification, was celebrated on June 1st in the German Democratic Republic.)

The 1.2.3 Farm receives the "Toy of the Year" award in the Netherlands—a distinction which the construction worker squad of 1975, the rescue helicopter of 1987, the Indian family of 1989 and the small Victorian house from 1990 all achieved previously.

In 1991, the Brandstätter corporate group generates profits totalling over 400 million Marks. The company has invested 350 million Marks over the last 20 years.

from the beginnings to the present day

The award-winning circus series provides endless possibilities for expansion.

92

from the beginnings to the present day

Bavaria's Interior Minister, Dr. Günther Beckstein, presents Horst Brandstätter with the Federal Cross of Merit on a ribbon.

 **1992**

For the first time, two catalogues are released in one year: a spring-summer catalogue and, in September, an autumn-winter catalogue. This is a necessary step, given that all print runs of the 1991–92 catalogue were exhausted by the end of 1991. One and a half million copies are printed for the German market alone. Parents name it as their children's favourite picture book, or their "Bible".

The "Tim's Adventure" colouring contest—in which children are asked to colour in a skier—draws 75,000 entries. Their industriousness is rewarded with additional group prizes for kindergartens.

PLAYMOBIL is sold in Moscow's famous GUM department store. In honour of the premiere, the life-sized PLAYMOBIL pirate captain himself makes the long journey and conquers Red Square.

In the "City Machine" adventure area at the International Exposition in Seville, blocks containing 1,800 PLAYMOBIL figures illustrate the population density of Germany. The PLAYMOBIL circus "Romani" receives the "Product of the Year 1992" award from the consumer plastic products association and the "Spiel gut" seal from the Arbeitsausschuss Kinderspiel und Spielzeug (task force for children's toys and games), as well as the "Oscar de Jouet"—the French toy "Oscar". The latter, by the way, marks the first time this award has been given to a toy manufactured outside of France.

 1993

The 1992–93 catalogue is a full 36 pages long. No wonder: Among other things, it has to introduce the new large knights' castle. In June, the third Children's Day at PLAYMOBIL attracts over 12,000 visitors to Zirndorf. Horst Brandstätter is awarded Germany's Federal Cross of Merit for his service to the public good, for fostering the employment market and for creating a corporate group with an international reputation.

The dentist's office helps PLAYMOBIL win the title of "Toy of the Year" in the Netherlands for the fifth time in seven years.

The young artist Kiki Ahlers premieres her installation Anita at the College of Visual Arts in Hamburg: 10,312 white PLAYMOBIL women and men stand row upon row; on the wall behind them are large photographs depicting an equal number of first names which are approved by the German civil registry office.

from the beginnings to the present day

PLAYMOBIL Specials are introduced onto the market with twelve different figures, ranging from a detective to a night watchman to a rock musician to Dracula. The little figure packages, priced to be given as small gifts, have since become a permanent part of the PLAYMOBIL assortment.

 1994

Hans Beck turns 65, but has no thoughts of retiring just yet.

PLAYMOBIL turns 20 years old. In 1994, more than 21 million PLAYMOBIL packages are delivered; the company records profits of 400 million Marks—63 percent of it through export.

PLAYMOBIL wins its suit against Carrera on all counts. The conflict began in 1991, when the Fürth-based toy manufacturer Carrera Century Toys brought its "play o.k." onto the market. The play o.k. figures' resemblance to PLAYMOBIL figures was reason enough for Brandstätter to file an action at the regional court of Nuremberg-Fürth. The Federal Court of Justice in Karlsruhe confirms the legal validity of the verdict passed on May 25, 1993. This means that Carrera is forbidden to manufacture or distribute the stiff-legged figures in question. In the meantime, Carrera had quickly produced a figure with legs which can be splayed, but PLAYMOBIL immediately files suit against this one as well.

The wandering monk, a character from the knights' series, is PLAYMOBIL's first religious figure.

 1995

The figure of the Axe Man (medieval executioner) is introduced, sparking a wave of protests. However, he is the embodiment of the justice system in the time of the knights, and therefore fits in with the series.

A record 63 new products come onto the market, including an entire fairy tale and fantasy world, complete with witch, fairies, dragon, flying carpet, wizard's workshop and dragon's temple.

In Korea, a department store collapses: 205 people are killed, 1000 are injured. After nearly ten days, the 21-year-old architecture student Choi is rescued alive. Groping around in his completely dark, rubble-filled dungeon with nothing to eat, he was only able to find a PLAYMOBIL 1.2.3 train and a puzzle box. According to his doctors, the fact that he could pass his time in isolation playing with the train contributed greatly to his ability to suppress his fear of death.

from the beginnings to the present day

from the beginnings to the present day

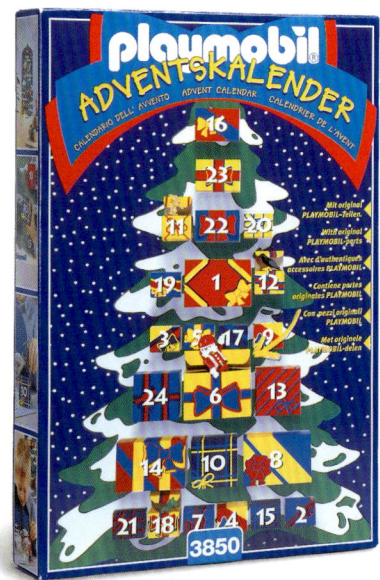

 1996

Horst Brandstätter founds the non-profit organisation, "Kinderförderung von PLAYMOBIL" (PLAYMOBIL's children's advancement foundation).

The fire-fighting vehicles are outfitted with flashing, battery-operated lights; a pressure pump allows children to pump water through the hoses. The fire departments of Zirndorf and Menden served as consultants to the development department on this project. Conversely, the real firefighters use the toy vehicles as fire safety teaching tools, to help demonstrate to children how to behave in an emergency.

Due to low sales, the monk is scheduled to be removed from the programme, a decision that sparks a storm of protest from the Bavarian and church-sponsored press. The orca whale surfaces in the season's programme. In order to manufacture it—using a combination of hard and flexible materials—the company invests 600,000 Marks in new injection moulds and machines. Thanks to a sinker weight and a hollow cavity, the whale can swim in two different positions—either with its entire back fin out of the water or only its head. In May, PLAYMOBIL launches its 500-page website.

For the first time, PLAYMOBIL introduces an Advent calendar. Initially, it is marketed exclusively in VEDES toy stores. Conceived of as an alternative to chocolate or hand-made calendars, it nevertheless requires the user's active participation: Before the first of December, the 24 little boxes need to be assembled, filled with PLAYMOBIL pieces and hung on the calendar. Then, little by little, in the days leading up to Christmas Eve, the child can put together an entire winter and Christmas-themed scene. The idea is so well received that Barbie, Baby Born, LEGO and other toy Advent calendars appear on the market soon afterwards. Eighty-five percent of PLAYMOBIL's exports go to other European countries; France remains the most important foreign market.

from the beginnings to the present day

 1997

After 15 years, the remote-controlled RC-Train takes the place of the toy train. The old, current-carrying metal tracks from LGB are replaced by new tracks made entirely of plastic. They can be laid down indoors or out and are completely weatherproof. The train runs on a rechargeable battery. The "train driver" can stand up to thirty feet away from the tracks and still control the train's movements precisely. The first houses are now built using "System X". The name refers to the small, X-shaped connecting pieces which hold the individual parts together. Its advertising slogan is "The trick with the click".

A new, much spiffier looking police car also comes onto the market. Out of consideration for parents, it has only a patrol light and no siren.

A black Corsair ship is released as a special, limited-edition product and is an enormous hit.

PLAYMOBIL processes the 100,000th ton of granulated plastic in its 23-year history. The supplier is Rey-Plastic GmbH in Hamburg.

To ensure that the new products are well publicised, this year's advertising budget is stepped up to 18 million Marks. A record 2.5 million copies of the PLAYMOBIL catalogue are printed.

Three of PLAYMOBIL's most avid collectors meet in Zirndorf: One of them is Erik Skaarup, a 26-year-old Norwegian baker and pastry maker who—with very few exceptions—owns every PLAYMOBIL item that has ever existed. The artist Men Rabe paints an alternative version of Tischbein's Goethe, the "PLAYMOBIL Goethe".

Horst Brandstätter is made an honorary citizen of his home town of Zirndorf.

Brandstätter finances the renovation of the stadium belonging to the 2nd Division soccer club Greuther Fürth, which is located on his property. The stadium is renamed PLAYMOBIL Stadium.

97

from the beginnings to the present day

 1998

After 40 years at PLAYMOBIL, Hans Beck retires.

The fairy tale castle arrives on the market, and, in cooperation with Ubi Soft in Düsseldorf, three CD-ROMs are released: Hype—The Time Quest, Laura's Happy Adventure (for girls aged six to ten) and Alex Builds His Farm for the little ones. The Franconian town of Bad Windsheim proves its status as a child-friendly shopping city by transforming itself into a PLAYMOBIL land during the Advent season. Toddler-sized PLAYMOBIL Santa Claus figures and PLAYMOBIL decorations are displayed in shop windows, squares and playgrounds.

In September in Zirndorf, the District Administrator of Fürth presents Theo Waigel, Germany's then-Minister of Finance, with the PLAYMOBIL gold mine from the Western town series to help him reduce the budget deficit.

A major Christmas campaign in Bad Windsheim: PLAYMOBIL Santa Clauses decorate every display window in town.

 1999

The 22,000 sq. ft. French version of the FunPark opens on the outskirts of Paris, modelled after the original in Zirndorf; it is nearly overrun by enthusiastic PLAYMOBIL fans. In Orlando, Florida, as well, a 4,500 sq. ft. FunPark opens in the Mall of Florida. Since Americans are especially hygiene-conscious, all the figures and accessories on the play tables need to be cleaned every day. So the Park makes the cleaning process fun, integrating a giant bull's eye window into the room, through which children can watch the little people go through the spin cycle.

PLAYMOBIL turns 25 and says "thank you" with a limited edition rescue boat and anniversary suitcases for the little ones. The company makes its second expedition outside the Earth's atmosphere with a new space series.
The farm has been freshly renovated and arrives with new spotted cows.

At the end of the year, a PLAYMOBIL crèche is introduced, including Mary, Joseph and Baby Jesus, complete with ox, donkey, sheep and shepherds. The response from the church is highly positive: According to a television survey, many children no longer know the reason why people celebrate Christmas or when Jesus' birthday is.
The BDU (Bund Deutscher Unternehmensberater = Association of German Management Consultants) selects Horst Brandstätter as its "Manager of the Year". Ironically, profits in this anniversary year drop from 450 million Marks down to 420 million. The dip is the result of problems with a new software system that controls production, leading to massive difficulties with delivery.
In Berlin, the exhibition Playart is opened, consisting of unusual works of art featuring the little people; Hans Beck is in attendance.

In a back courtyard in Berlin's trendy Prenzlauer Berg neighbourhood, this entrance welcomes curious visitors to an unusual exhibition.

from the beginnings to the present day

PLAYMOBIL First Smile:
For a smile from the start.

100

from the beginnings to the present day

2000

At the EXPO 2000, Hans Beck is honoured as one of 47 Germans who have had a positive influence on the nation. His bust, carried by three large PLAYMOBIL figures, stands in the Idea Workshop in the German Pavilion, alongside Boris Becker, Johann Wolfgang von Goethe and Alice Schwarzer.
Following an eight-week-long trial period during the previous summer, the outdoor area of the 1,000,000 sq. ft. PLAYMOBIL FunPark in Zirndorf is now officially opened. Lechuza, a line of self-watering plant containers is launched as a new sector of geobra Brandstätter GmbH & Co. KG. The product was invented by the boss himself. The pirate ship is released onto the market with a new look, as a pirate flagship. PLAYMOBIL's baby product line, First Smile, with the slogan "For a smile from the start" aims to establish brand loyalty very early. A decorative chain of PLAYMOBIL figures for the baby carriage can be followed, starting at the age of 3 months, by the rattle.
Florian Illies, editor of the Frankfurter Allgemeine Zeitung and a first-generation PLAYMOBIL child, pays a literary tribute to his favourite toy in the best-selling book, Generation Golf: "I'm feeling good. It's Saturday evening, I'm sitting in the warm bathtub, and my brown PLAYMOBIL pirate ship is floating through the soap bubbles. Later, [the popular variety quiz show] Wetten, dass...? is on TV, with Frank Elstner. In other words: I feel as though the postman had just delivered me a worry-free-in-every-way package." Thus begins Illies's look back at the 1980s.

2001

The geobra Brandstätter company celebrates its 125th anniversary.
PLAYMOBIL assumes 100 percent control of its manufacturing facilities in Spain. The Eastern European region is left out of the firm's expansion plans for the time being. "Our company philosophy demands that we meet high expectations as far as play value and quality are concerned. A prerequisite for this is a certain level of parental income. Therefore, we still need to move carefully in this region," explains distribution chief Oswald Bayer.
The PLAYMOBIL FunPark is expanded to include an Indian village and a golf driving range.
In the wake of the remote-controlled train, the first vehicles with an optional remote control module set come onto the market. The big autumn and Christmas theme is the

jet airliner and airport, which—of all possible times—arrive in the stores in September. But the horrible events of September 11th do not affect the popularity of the airliner and tower. On the contrary, say educators, they may even help children cope with what they have seen. In any event, the jet airliner is completely sold out by Christmas. Another highlight worth mentioning is the speedboat, which was a similarly huge hit in the summertime.

from the beginnings to the present

 2002

Germany's firefighters receive new grey uniforms; naturally, their PLAYMOBIL colleagues have to follow suit.

At the same time, the fire-fighting vehicle fleet is updated with a rescue equipment truck, an equipment trailer with floodlights and a fire chief's car. German fire departments praise the realistic depiction of the protective clothing and equipment.

And a prize follows immediately: The magazine Familie & Co. presents the PLAYMOBIL "Fire Department" play world with its "Golden Rocking-horse" award in the category "For Artists and Handcrafters". The toy series is particularly praised for its loving attention to detail, numerous expansion options and the communication of positive values.

In the USA, a special firefighter figure is released—the "FDNY Fire Fighter". A portion of the profits from its sale go to the NYC Fire Department, which has become even more beloved by the public since the events of September 11, 2001.

The familiar old shops are replaced by the new PLAYMOBIL grocery store set, which soon tops many children's wish lists. Only the parents are easily frustrated by the labels that need to be stuck onto pickle jars, milk cartons and ketchup bottles. PLAYMOBIL recognises the problem quickly, and in later years, the labels are put on at the factory.

After centuries of wandering, the Vikings finally reach Zirndorf and take the PLAYMOBIL fans by storm. Supersets are another completely new item. Depending on the theme in question, children can use a base platform included in the package to plant vegetables, install pipes under the street or bury treasure. In addition, all PLAYMOBIL packages now display their contents clearly on the back.

Even little children are spared doing strenuous work: The 1.2.3 preschool train set has a battery operated locomotive so that children no longer have to push it along.

On May 11 and 12, the production department in Dietenhofen holds an open house. 25,000 visitors come to learn about how their favourite toys are made.

At the FunPark, visitors are thrilled by the gold and precious stone mine. Directly across from the park, the apart-hotel PLAYMOBIL Inn opens, with 28 family suites; during the tourist season, it is fully booked almost every day.

Thanks to a raffle held at the FunPark, PLAYMOBIL is able to donate 500,000 Euros to help the child protection agency in the district of Döbeln rebuild a playground which was completely destroyed in the year's floods.

Prospecting for gold at the PLAYMOBIL FunPark

from the beginnings to the present day

from the beginnings to the present day

 2003

In the hot summer of 2003, when temperatures in Germany reach over 100 °F, the PLAYMOBIL figures are also able to go swimming. The residents of the modern house build a swimming pool in their garden, complete with a functioning shower (item 3205). Developers had been trying to realise this theme for a long time: The problem which always arose was that the figures could not undress completely, nor should they go swimming fully clothed. The dilemma was solved by giving the little people short leggings and T-shirts. Naturally, they can take off their flip-flops beforehand.

The Western and space series are removed from the programme, but some pieces are still available via direct mail order.

This year's Christmas highlights come onto the market in the form of the electric crane and Noah's ark. Crane and ark parts are moulded around the clock. Three months before Christmas, the entire production runs of both items have been sold to distributors.

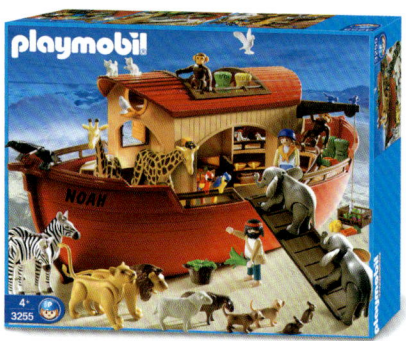

The skeleton of the indoor event centre is completed on the grounds of the FunPark. The building will provide play areas, spaces for events and performances and dining facilities even in winter or in bad weather, and will cost around 50 million Euros.
In Herne, Westphalia, the first collectors' market attracts approximately 90 visitors from Germany and neighbouring countries to the city's event centre. An especially sought-after item: blister packages from 1974, PLAYMOBIL's first year.
On November 30, the Museum of Palatinate History in Speyer opens the successful family exhibition, 30 Years of Playmobil—Discover the World, covering a space of 17,500 sq. ft.

 2004

In celebration of PLAYMOBIL's 30th birthday, two official anniversary items are presented at the International Toy Fair in Nuremberg: The "Western Classic Set", in original 1970s style, and the "Golden Knight". If we compare the very first PLAYMOBIL knights with this magnificent birthday well-wisher, the evolution of the product is clearly visible. Yet the figure's face and body size are exactly the same as they were three decades earlier.
Finally, there are dinosaurs at PLAYMOBIL as well. Long wished-for by children, they could not be worked into the programme due to their size and historical context. Developers finally solve the problem by letting scientists discover dinosaurs and skeletons frozen in the ice.

from the beginnings to the present day

PLAYMOBIL celebrates its 30th birthday with these two special edition items.

A lion in the jail,
or what would today's children play with if there were no PLAYMOBIL?

The firefighters bravely put out the blaze in the trunk of the getaway car; the construction workers are invited for tea at the farm, since they are building a street in another part of the playroom; and the police try to capture the bison that has escaped from the stable. The police boat officers board the pirate ship, and the bike policeman patrols the zoo looking for the motorbike hooligan who crashed the gates with his chopper. The monkey's keeper has fallen from a tree and needs to be picked up by the rescue helicopter; and in the PLAYMOBIL house, sleeping places have to be found for ten children.

PLAYMOBIL leaves its mark

PLAYMOBIL: The LEGO generation initially viewed it with contempt: "Everything is done for you—you can't change anything and there's hardly anything to build." Yet every day, our children show us how mistaken this attitude can be. The construction of a play scenario can take up an entire morning. And everything that comes in the PLAYMOBIL box gets used. A shark could even show up in a garden pond. And even if the first generation of PLAYMOBIL players complain today that printing has made the figures too specific, children's imaginations still know no bounds.

"PLAYMOBIL is great"—children, parents and educators all agree on this point. Beginning with the first test children to whom Hans Beck gave his prototypes, he, at least, knew: "This is good". 26 years and millions of PLAYMOBIL figures later, Florian Illies, author and editor of the Frankfurter Allgemeine Zeitung, paid a literary tribute to the little people: "We could devote ourselves to what was essential. That is: Play with PLAYMOBIL. PLAYMOBIL is, without a doubt, the most formative thing that occurred in our generation," he explains in Generation Golf, an examination of the 1980s. (The reference is to the Volkswagen Golf, an extremely popular car at that time.) And Trixi—born in 1967 and thus a member of the Golf generation—wrote to PLAYMOBIL at the age of 16: "I want to write down the reasons why your toy has fascinated me so much. On the one hand, it imitates everything truthfully; but at the same time, it is created to appeal to children. It doesn't look too grown up, yet it is not too cute either. Everything is simply picturesque: The colours are so diverse, the details are so carefully thought out, the size is not clumsy. And it is these very things that fill the toy with so much life..."

It started with the idea of making a toy available which would give children joy not just once, but again and again—that is, a play system. Building blocks of every sort already existed. What was missing were figures with which children could re-enact everything they experience and everything that interests them—for hours on end. PLAYMOBIL lets you explore everything your imagination will allow.

ANYTHING IS POSSIBLE

"Your child can transpose the natural adult environment into the small world of the playroom. Using all of his imagination, he can build an amazingly authentic re-creation of reality. The simple, child-friendly design of the figures and accessories virtually challenges children to actively create." In 1974, the brochure that accompanied the first PLAYMOBIL toys explained their meaning and purpose to uninformed parents. But thanks to the manageable figures, children could not only re-enact the real world, they could finally be everything that they dreamed of. "Once upon a time there was a little girl. Like all little girls, she dreamed of a knight in shining armour, riding on a magnificent horse, who took her with him to his castle and made her his

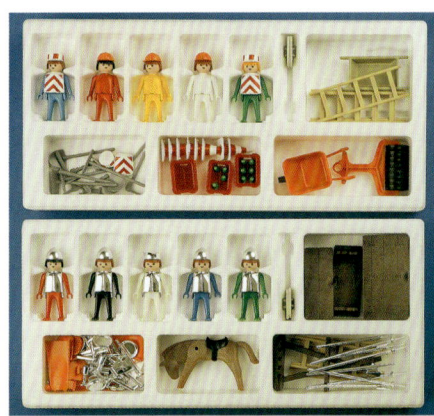

PLAYMOBIL imagined the toys being organised like this; the reality is quite a bit wilder. And of course you need a bathtub to test whether or not the pirate ship really floats.

PLAYMOBIL leaves its mark

If you couldn't afford the Western buildings, you simply made your own: "I built myself a much nicer Western fort out of wood and cardboard," says Jens, 33—aged six to 13 at the time.

princess. The little girl also passionately wished to go to the circus and become a wild animal trainer. In fact, she just wanted to have lots and lots of animals—preferably a whole zoo. And then one day it happened! One day, a man named Beck came along and invented the world in which the little girl's dreams would be fulfilled." These are the reminiscences of Daniela Schabenstiel, an avid PLAYMOBIL player, and now an equally passionate collector.

PLAYMOBIL—it's the whole world on a dollhouse scale. It is small enough that the entire Western town can fit into a child's room, yet big enough that you can really give the horse a drink or set the table in the saloon with plates, knives and forks.

Here, there are no grown-up rules that say you can't put a bed in the garden or a cow inside the house. For children, cars can simply fly up to the second floor of the parking garage—and the same is true with PLAYMOBIL. The child decides what and how to play. Finally, she can make the rules: She is no longer on the lowest rung of the adult hierarchy, having to submit to her parents' rules. Be it a zoo director, robber-knight, damsel of the castle or police officer—in PLAYMOBIL Land, you can be anything and do anything. Thanks to the way that the figures were initially conceived, this could happen at lightning speed, so that, at the end of his day's work, the construction worker could become a knight. And if he got bored with that, he could put on his

PLAYMOBIL leaves its mark

"We had the circus. We played circus with our pets (hamster and rabbit), and tried to teach them to do tricks," remembers Manuel, now 24—aged three to ten during his period of cruelty to animals.

"I have a PLAYMOBIL aeroplane and 300 building blocks. I build towers with them and replay the collapse of the World Trade Center," says Mirko, age eight.

Indian trappings and paddle away in his canoe. Nowadays, the play worlds are more extensive, and, thanks to the PLAYMOBIL catalogue, children's wishes are getting bigger and bigger. Wouldn't it be wonderful to have the whole zoo that's depicted in the beautiful double-page spread? ...Yes, it would be—but you can also do it much more simply. If you have a few animals and the right surface, you can do without the zoo buildings.

"I liked playing with animals best of all, even outdoors. I always arranged them so that they wouldn't be able to eat each other up. But it was still important that every animal got enough to eat. They had to make do with grass and hay from my guinea pig cage; even the dogs and the lions got it. When I played circus, I brought out carpet squares, so that the animals would also know where the ring was," says Jenny, age 30, describing her zookeeper phase between the ages of five and 13. The examples shown on the package or in a three-dimensional display in a toy store window represent the way adults would imagine a farm assembled by a child. But the way a child actually plays might look very different. This, for PLAYMOBIL, is the very purpose of the toy, as Hans Beck emphatically states: "We don't design scenarios; at most, we give suggestions on the packages and in the brochures. We don't want to communicate a specific image to the children. We are giving them materials for creative play. Every child will do something different with it. There are so many factors that influence this over which we have no control: age, stage of development, parents' socio-economic status, siblings, school, friends and other stimuli." Naturally, children don't only re-create peaceful scenarios or idealised worlds. They can also use PLAYMOBIL to play out scenes of destruction or work through childish fears of characters such as robbers. When the airport series arrived on the market in the autumn of 2001, of all times, one might have thought that very few people would want to buy it. After all, who would want to give a child a jet airliner for Christmas in the immediate wake of the horrible events of September 11? But in fact, the reverse was true: The jet airliner was a best-seller, and children used it to work through the events they had been exposed to in the media. For one thing, the toy provided the invaluable advantage of allowing the stories to turn out quite differently...

111

PLAYMOBIL leaves its mark

BECAUSE ONE THING FITS WITH ANOTHER

"Where should the farm family sleep?" wonders seven-year-old Frederike, setting the beds from the camper up in the hayloft and adding the stove from the PLAYMOBIL house along with them. Only the refrigerator-freezer won't fit under the slanted roof. She sets the table in front of the barn, and the turtle swims in a pond that actually belongs to the modern house. "Because one thing fits with another"—children have understood this concept from the very beginning. All of the figures fit into every vehicle, on horses or on the trapeze. Even today, when the figures are printed or dressed more specifically, this feature has not changed. Only a few parents, who have spent three hours on Christmas Eve assembling a police station or a supermarket are slightly put out when, on Christmas Day, the animal hospital has already moved into the building and the jail is being used as a recovery cage for the sick lion. But the logic of parents is completely out of place here.

HOW AND WHAT DO YOU PLAY WITH PLAYMOBIL?

You can play just about anything with PLAYMOBIL. Many adults remember their personal PLAYMOBIL stories very vividly and fondly. When asked how and what they played with PLAYMOBIL—or how they play with it now—large and small PLAYMOBIL fans responded as follows:

"I played at the home of my friends Maren and Vera—and with at least five or six other kids—just about everything, as long as the Western world was involved. We combined it with everything else we had in our rooms: LEGO, stuffed animals, Barbies, etc." says Stephanie, age 30, whose Western craze lasted from the ages of five to ten.

"I usually played with it by myself; I could occupy myself with it for hours at a time. But I also played PLAYMOBIL with friends: For example, with my camper in the garden. We cooked ant soup in the PLAYMOBIL camp cooking pot. Very creative... I especially liked the hundred thousand little accessories and details. I could constantly arrange and rearrange my pots and soup ladles inside the camper. Of course, after every drive, everything was a mess again—probably just like it is in real life," remembers Iris, age 30, a camping fanatic from ages four to eleven.

"I mostly played with my brother, who was seven years older. Usually we built a city where each of us had certain houses and each of us played with certain people. In order to combine all of the play worlds, we built a theme park that tourists could travel through on the big ferry boat while actors played out scenarios in the different theme areas. That way, we could set up the Wild West, the knights, the pirate world and even the North Pole, all side by side," recounts Sven, who was between three and eleven years old at the time. Today, he is 25 years old and has become a collector.

"I make up stories and pretend that the PLAYMOBIL people can talk," says Carla, age seven.

"I played building contractor and hospital with my friend. We combined the toys with wooden building blocks and metal toys for outdoors in the sandbox," says Gerrit, age 36. He worked as a building contractor from age eight to eleven; today, he is an architect.

Educators were also impressed with PLAYMOBIL from the very beginning. Remedial teachers, psychologists, schools inspectors, occupational therapists and preschool teachers agreed: PLAYMOBIL stimulates the imagination, develops fine motor skills, encourages role-playing and independent play and provides unlimited stimuli for learning about one's environment. In addition, "it requires very little storage space," attested a Munich kindergarten in 1977. Opinions on this issue would probably differ today. But for some time now, PLAYMOBIL has ceased to be an unusual toy found only in kindergartens: Rather, it is a standard feature of almost every German playroom. In order to support educators' enthusiasm—and perhaps to expose even more children to PLAYMOBIL—from 1986 to 1996, PLAYMOBIL even produced packages especially for kindergartens which contained domestic and exotic animals as well as a set of 33 figures and accessories from daily life, from wheelchairs to skateboards.

By now, adults are also well aware of the value of PLAYMOBIL. On his late-night talk show, host Harald Schmidt re-enacted international political events using PLAYMOBIL—from Trozki's flight to Switzerland, to the first moon landing and the fall of the Berlin Wall, to the story-lines of operas and novels such as the Ring of the Nibelung or Kafka's Metamorphosis. The TV news magazine ZDF Heute Journal once explained the structure of the new European Parliament using the little figures, and the little people are even found in management training. What does it mean if, at the beginning of a group-building seminar, you select a firefighter or a police officer? Is it depth psychology or just a childhood trauma—like Gerrit's, for example: "I got the garbage truck for Christmas, when what I'd really wished for was the dump truck."

WHAT SPRINGS TO MIND ABOUT PLAYMOBIL

We could no longer even imagine a world without PLAYMOBIL. When asked about their experiences with the toy, these are some of the answers that children and adults gave to the question, "What else springs to mind when you think about PLAYMOBIL?"

"A lovely toy; I have happy memories of that time—it kept us quiet for hours." —Edith, age 38.

"My childhood without PLAYMOBIL: I can't imagine it!" —Iris, age 30.

"That it's fun." —Lisa, age eight.

"Now my nephew plays with it with just the same enthusiasm, especially with the knights' castle—made of our old things combined with newly-purchased ones." —Sabine, age 33.

"That PLAYMOBIL is great." —Lea, age eight.

"A wonderful toy! It's still fun for me at my advanced age." —Dagmar, age 39.

"You were always losing the little things and the accessories, but it was still a great toy." —Jörg, age 30.

"I would still buy PLAYMOBIL for myself now; my enthusiasm hasn't waned." —Bettina, age 23.

"The products are getting better all the time, but they're also becoming less flexible. Nowadays, you can't demote a police officer to a construction worker's job as easily. Today's kids may be robbed of some of their imagination, since they get everything pre-processed." —Jens, age 33.

"Thanks to Hans Beck for the best invention in the world!!" —Andreas, age 35.

PLAYMOBIL leaves its mark

Caution: Too much PLAYMOBIL may be dangerous to your health! Eventually, the little people might band together and fight back—like in this scene from Gulliver's Travels, an entry in a photo contest sponsored by PLAYMOBIL.

PLAYMOBIL TRADITIONS

Hans Beck established three maxims which, more or a tiny bit less, are still in effect today:

No violence or horror scenarios

Well, the cowboys were quickly equipped with Colts and the Indians with bows and arrows. After all, these accessories are part of the image that we have of cowboys and Indians—and in our not always peaceful world, the re-enactment of violent scenes is a part of life. However, children do not necessarily associate the pirate ship's plastic cannon balls or the knights' battering ram with death and mutilation. Of course, one group of knights loses the battle, but you can bet that they will all celebrate together afterwards—or at least, the next fight will end differently. Furthermore—and we have to be honest about this—the competing PlayBIG figures enticed children from the very beginning with entire arsenals of weapons. But modern weapons of mass destruction, fighter planes and tanks will never be seen at PLAYMOBIL.

No imitations of short-lived trends

Of course, it would be easy for geobra Brandstätter to recreate Bob the Builder and his fleet of work vehicles in PLAYMOBIL or to build a System X version of Harry Potter's Hogwarts School. But not only does Horst Brandstätter prefer to put his own ideas on the market, free of budget-gobbling licensing fees, but such products would also limit children's imaginations when playing with them.

No automated toys

A child should push a car along, and not simply watch a car drive by. PLAYMOBIL does make remote controlled vehicles now, but they still demand a lot of fine motor skill. Furthermore, they are initially delivered without the motors, and can also be played with this way. Flashing lights on police cars, fire engines and flatbed trucks are now battery operated, but the toys still spare children's tender ears and parents' sensitive nerves from howling sirens. The only two PLAYMOBIL items which can make sounds are the piano (item 5551) from the dollhouse series—which plays Für Elise—

and the organ grinder (item 5500), also from the pink collection. Nowadays, the Christmas tree lights up, and the crane rotates at the touch of a button and lifts the construction crew's office using its battery-powered engine. Naturally, the toy train which arrived on the market in 1980 ran on electricity from the very beginning (using transformers until 1997; later remote controlled with rechargeable batteries). The various boats—and even the sea serpent—can swim across the bathtub or wading pool on their own, using an underwater motor; but they can just as easily be pushed across the carpet by hand.

WHAT DO YOU (OR DID YOU) LIKE BEST ABOUT PLAYMOBIL?

The question of what people like or liked most about PLAYMOBIL prompts a wide variety of answers:

Children

- that you can put things together according to your own imagination
- that you can set things up in any position
- that they are bigger than LEGO
- it's fun
- that the figures can move their hands
- that there are so many different items
- that you can always invent new stories and set them up differently every time
- everything looks nice

Adults

- the widely varied themes, executed simply and attractively—giving you the opportunity to develop your own stories, to set them up, and then to play with them
- all the animals and people were friendly and looked friendly
- the details (weapons, pitchers)
- the pirate ship was nicer-looking than the LEGO one
- that the figures all somehow fit together as far as size and design were concerned; a miniature world where the scale always stays the same
- the friendly-looking faces
- sturdy, indestructible; you can even play with them outdoors
- nice and colourful; lots of different individual pieces
- the opportunity to put it together yourself

WHAT IS OR WAS NOT SO GREAT ABOUT PLAYMOBIL?

But of course, there are two sides to every coin. There were and are aspects of PLAYMOBIL which have not met with wide approval:

Children

- that you always have to pick it up afterwards
- that they can't switch bodies like the LEGO figures
- that PLAYMOBIL people's movements are not very flexible
- that the figures can get lost easily
- the cars
- that you can't take off the figures' clothes and dress them in something else
- that it takes so long to set up
- that they are so hard

Adults

- that the figures themselves were very limited in their mobility and that due to their hairstyles (because of hats), the heads were quite unnatural and misshapen looking
- constant new products; you could never stay up to date
- unfortunately, back then, they couldn't move their hands
- the people were always grinning, no matter what you did with them
- when the figures' hands broke off, they couldn't hold anything anymore
- the horses' heads sometimes wore out after a while, and then they could only graze
- the people's hats always fell off too easily
- PLAYMOBIL must have really been expensive: You could always tell who was rich by the size of their fire engine

"I liked playing with the fire engine the best. Unfortunately, I just had the little truck—the big one was too expensive."
—Britta, age 33, fighting fires from ages seven to ten.

PLAYMOBIL leaves its mark

Despite the drawbacks mentioned above, the PLAYMOBIL world has remained wholesome to this day—even when enemy knights storm the castle or the pirates shoot their cannons. The figures have not stopped smiling yet.

"I'm now 20 years old; I and my brother, who is now 18, used to play with PLAYMOBIL a lot and we had lots of it. We kept it in boxes, and since it had gotten pretty dusty in there, I recently put the pieces through the dishwasher, which they survived very well. While doing this, I—honestly—got the urge to play with them again! The quality of your toys is really very good; they haven't lost their colour even after more than ten years, and they even survived the dishwasher. By the way, my favourite thing to play with was the Indians." —Caroline R. (2002)

"The PLAYMOBIL catalogue is my three-year-old son's current bedtime reading material. He's already used it to 'write' a wish list for Santa Claus, including the police van, getaway car and safe crackers. His grandmother had wanted to get a Carrera racetrack instead, but Junior only wants these three products from PLAYMOBIL—you can't change his mind."
—Gabi R. (2002)

"Hi there! You did a great job with this new addition to the 'Fire Department' series! The authenticity of the—as we firefighters say—'personal protection equipment' (breathing protection), and the hazardous material protection suit is excellent! Also as far as the emergency vehicles are concerned: Well thought-out solutions that the standards committee ought to take a look at (rescue equipment trailer)!"
—Michael B., volunteer fire department, Nübbel (2002)

117

IN THE LAND OF SMILES—NOBODY IS REALLY EVIL

"At first, we didn't include any warlike characteristics. It was only in the second year that we gave bows and arrows to the PLAYMOBIL Indians and rifles and Colts to the cowboys," says Hans Beck, remembering the pacifist era at PLAYMOBIL.

If it had been up to him, his play world would have remained completely idealistic. But he gave in to current trends and designed knives, daggers, swords, sabres, pistols, axes, flails, bows and arrows, crossbows, battering rams, slingshots, assault towers for the knights' castle and cannons for the pirate ship. The latter, equipped with a release spring and little plastic cannon balls, can shoot an impressive 12 inches across the playroom—which doesn't really bother any of the PLAYMOBIL figures, since they seldom get knocked down. To do that, you need to bring in the "Big Bertha" cannon with its ping-pong sized balls. Only the Americans are afraid that enraged parents could file lawsuits for millions of dollars: Therefore, the little cannon balls can't really be fired there. After all, Junior could shoot himself in the nose with a plastic ball or hit his best friend in the eye. But Big Bertha is considered non-dangerous in the USA: Nobody's nostrils are that big.

PLAYMOBIL is not interested in senseless violence, but the people who create the world in miniature realise that violence is also a part of it. "Children are almost magically attracted to militant subjects like pirates, knights and the Old West," Hans Beck explained more than ten years ago. "This is not because they enjoy senseless brutality, but because they can use these scenarios very well to deal with their own situation. Being weak and powerless against the adult world is one of the primary experiences of childhood. That's why they like so much to be strong, powerful and brave." But not in the style of Rambo; rather, in a historical or social framework, as in the case of knights or police officers. PLAYMOBIL saw the introduction of the axe man in 1995 in this same historical context. "In the Middle Ages, the executioner was the representative of the law; beheadings were meant to be a deterrent. It was a spontaneous idea; I thought it was funny. I toned him down and made him slightly grotesque with his lopped-off pointy hood. Everyone who saw him had to smile," says Hans Beck, defending the figure which, outside the walls of PLAYMOBIL, did not always get a jovial reaction. But other items were also met with protest, such as the medieval hunting party with a wild boar on a spit, the trappers or the travelling performers with their dancing bear. People thought these depictions were too cruel. Even today, the PLAYMOBIL makers are still convinced that horror and violence have no place in the land of smiles. However, the definition of violence usually refers to war toys. Even though, in the late 1950s and early 1960s, geobra manufactured and sold Revell-style model V2 rocket kits, the production of soldiers, jeeps or tanks was really never considered in the case of PLAYMOBIL. "We, the Brandstätter company, take the position that war toys do not belong in the hands of children. With PLAYMOBIL, we present children with a reassuring, friendly world, which each child can design according to his needs and feelings. Winchesters and bows and arrows are simply a part of the Indian world. At any rate, there is a big difference between historical weapons like those at PLAYMOBIL and mod-

People lose their sense of humour when it comes to animals: Rather than protesting against pistols and cannons, adults were incensed by the hunting party and the medieval dancing bear.

"I mainly played with the knights' castle and with my sister. The most important thing was always setting up the city/castle, and arranging the 'living conditions'," says Sabine, now 33. And the castle theme has lost none of its attractiveness, even more than three decades after the invention of PLAYMOBIL: "My favourite thing is playing what it used to be like in a castle," says Kevin, age eleven.

ern machines of destruction," stated Horst Brandstätter in 1978.

The lists that PLAYMOBIL keeps every year, which meticulously record all the expansion ideas suggested by boys, girls and adults, show the recommendations "tank" and "soldiers" to be clear front runners, followed by a "special police task force". But this doesn't bother the PLAYMOBIL makers at all. Naturally, the police officers are armed, and they chase the safe crackers or the robbers who just helped their buddy escape from jail—but they will never carry machine guns. And the decision as to who wins in the end—the robbers or the police—is left up to the child. Quite frequently, the situation ends peacefully, with the semi-bad people realising that they've done wrong or with the pirates who attacked the castle deciding to have a party with the knights.

"BLUE FOR BOYS AND PINK FOR GIRLS"—
OR, HOW ARE WOMEN'S ROLES DEPICTED AT PLAYMOBIL?

The first generation of PLAYMOBIL figures: They were construction workers, knights and Indians. Not only the competition from the PlayBIG figures—which arrived on the market one year later with both male and female figures—but also numerous letters got the toy makers pondering. "At any rate, when I was playing with them, I noticed that there were only 'men'. Wouldn't it be possible to make an Indian mother and children for the Indian series, for example? Then you would be able to expand the game further," wrote Gudrun J. in 1975. PLAYMOBIL's creators quickly recognised that women were lacking, and they went into production in 1976. The only difference in the basic figure was in the top half of the body—which now looks like a loose smock or a micro-miniskirt—and in the hairstyle. Beginning in 1989, the women were actually given a female bosom, and by now, some even have eyelashes, rouge and high-heeled shoes. The stylish PLAYMOBIL woman wears a ponytail, braids, a bun or a pageboy cut—but the real trick is not to lose the minuscule hair ribbons. Clothing styles include short or long trousers or long skirts. Gowns and aprons can be clicked on and off. All kinds of hats, caps, tiaras, crowns and bonnets have now found their way into the PLAYMOBIL fashion museum as well.

They started at PLAYMOBIL as castle damsels, travellers, riders, Indians and housewives and worked their way slowly upward. In the second police series, in 1997,

women appeared in civil service as police officers; two years later, they flew along to meet the aliens in space. And some little tots base their knowledge of society on the world of PLAYMOBIL. When Daddy reads an article about firefighter training in the newspaper over breakfast, he wonders whether there are actually any female firefighters. The answer comes out of his five-year-old son like a pistol shot: "Of course there are. I have one from PLAYMOBIL." But it wasn't always like this: Mail carriers and nurses are typical women's professions, but—just as in real life—women are not tolerated on a construction site. In the historical scenarios, women are damsels of the castle, market sellers, maids, saloon girls with red-painted lips or farmers.

PLAYMOBIL women can work as teachers, television reporters, nurses, service station attendants or veterinarians. They perform in the circus, go diving, play tennis and golf, snowboard, paddle kayaks through rapids and sail catamarans. In 1999, the women finally got their own vehicle—the economy car. Now Mummy Gabrielle—identified by the printing on her sporty dress—can drive with her child and her dachshund to buy bottled water: The crate of bottles is in the back of the car. Women also rode in cars in the past, but always—at least in the brochures—in the passenger seat.

In 1976, the men finally got some female support.

Over the years, the PLAYMOBIL women have become more and more active. Alongside the classic female profession of schoolteacher, the veterinarian was added in 1997.

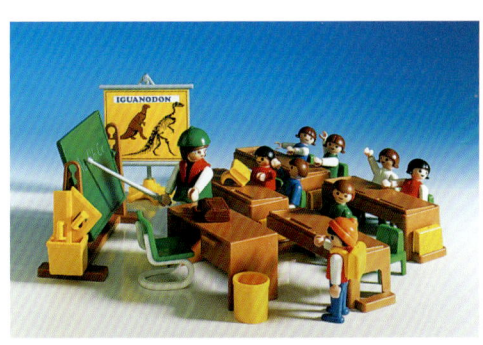

PLAYMOBIL leaves its mark

How strong the PLAYMOBIL women are allowed to be depends upon whether their roles are historical or contemporary. The PLAYMOBIL woman pirate —already in the collection since 1990—is not exactly prim and proper. By now, her great-granddaughter has asserted herself at home, taking photos of the outing while Daddy dutifully pushes the stroller.

STRONG WOMEN—NOT ONLY MADE OF PLAYMOBIL

They appeared in the fantasy adventures as fairies, witches and evil queens. As Viking women, they cooked the meals and took care of the children: logical so far. Considering this quite traditional development and distribution of roles, it is surprising that the first female pirate set sail at PLAYMOBIL as early as 1990. Ten years later, when the pirate ship was updated, she acquired a female colleague to guard the treasure at the lagoon. And anyone who wanted more could buy a female pirate as a Special beginning in 2003.

Even though many roles at PLAYMOBIL are still gender-specific—for example, the laundry room with a female figure and the lawnmower with a male—women's emancipation is gradually becoming more evident. Just as in real life at the company—where Andrea Schauer, Horst Brandstätter's emphatic personal choice, has been in charge of management since 2000—the jet airliner is now being flown by a male pilot and female copilot. And in the spring 2004 catalogue, the men were still doing the grilling and the women were changing diapers—but nevertheless, Daddy was loading the washing machine and pushing the stroller.

The male pilot and female copilot arrived on the market in 2001.

PLAYMOBIL leaves its mark

Gisela Kupiak has been the firm's press spokesperson since 1976. At the time that she interviewed for the position, she lived across from the factory, but she had very little idea of what geobra Brandstätter actually manufactured, and she had never even heard of PLAYMOBIL. Today, she is PLAYMOBIL history personified and knows everything that has happened over the course of her long career. She is always ready to lend an ear and offer an answer to journalists, to every question from customers or children and to the concerns and requests of the product's many collectors and fans. Not one of the letters or e-mails which arrive at the company every year goes unanswered. When the requests for individual and replacement parts began to get out of control, leading to the founding of the Direct Service department in 1982, she initially took charge of that area as well.

Andrea Schauer was not a PLAYMOBIL child herself. But her younger brother's enthusiasm for the product had already convinced her that it was a very special toy. And above all, when her own son began to play with it as well, she discovered how much creativity lay behind the system. Beginning in 1992, the trained political economist channelled her own positive experiences at the firm into the advertising and sales promotion departments. She was later promoted to head of marketing, and in the year 2000, company chief Horst Brandstätter appointed her Executive Director of Development, Marketing and Sales. In the beginning, she was not overjoyed: "Continuing his life's work seemed like an overwhelming task to me. And the idea of being responsible for 2000 employees also scared me off at first," the 47-year-old Schauer admits—but she has long since gotten used to it. In order to know exactly what she is marketing, by the way, she personally tests every new product.

Helga Ellul is the queen of Malta—at least of PLAYMOBIL Malta. In 1974, when she was 20 years old, Horst Brandstätter sent her off in her rickety Beetle from her hometown of Zirndorf to the faraway island to check the wage accounting for his 50 employees there. The short trip led her to the love of her life, and the little PLAYMOBIL people became her life's work. Today, she is in charge of 750 employees. She lives in the mini state with her husband, daughter, son and lots of pets. In addition to her job at PLAYMOBIL, she is also Vice President of the Chamber of Commerce and Industry and has an Order of Merit of the Republic of Malta at home in her jewellery box.

IS PLAYMOBIL A TOY FOR BOYS?

For the people in charge at PLAYMOBIL, an even more important subject than the role of women is children's playing behaviour. Even though PLAYMOBIL was not conceived of as a gender-specific toy, in practice, it has been shown that approximately three-quarters of its true fans are boys. After the first 15 years of PLAYMOBIL—in which the collection did consist of primarily male-dominated themes—a product line especially for girls was introduced onto the market. With the first 1900 series—later renamed the "PLAYMOBIL Dollhouse"—which, with its pink packaging, was explicitly aimed at girls—the company attempted to win over a new target group. Here, the design, details and characteristics are particularly pronounced. With the toy's historical placement at the turn of the twentieth century, Hans Beck saw the best opportunity to bring poetic, fairy tale-like touches into play: "This time period exuded more warmth than the modern world." In order not to leave boys out in the cold, the 1900 series initially included lots of extras such as vehicles, carriages and market stands. In 1998, the fairy tale castle joined the collection, in glittering pink gingerbread style—once again, intended primarily for girls. The modern house and the supermarket set—and an update of earlier grocery stores—are also focused around girl-specific content, but the subject matter is broad enough to appeal to boys as well. Naturally, many of the themes are still male-oriented, such as the construction site, for example—which is probably not at the top of many girls' wish lists—and the knights' castle. Instead, the designers are careful to include a token woman in the other scenarios: An adventurous girl plays in the tree house, for instance. Play worlds like the zoo, farm or Noah's ark are designed to appeal to animal-loving children of both sexes. The airport is also gender-neutral, since all children like to go on holidays.

The 1900 series was introduced onto the market in pink packaging especially for girls. Actually, this wasn't even necessary, since: "My favourite thing to play with is the PLAYMOBIL grocery store, and with my brother's police station," says Tabea, age eight.

SEVEN ARGUMENTS IN FAVOUR OF PLAYMOBIL

PLAYMOBIL keeps children quiet.
Provide one box of PLAYMOBIL, and the playroom won't exactly be tidy, but children will be diligently occupied for one to several hours.

PLAYMOBIL sharpens your vision.
Anyone who has ever tried to vacuum a dark blue carpet despite the presence of a PLAYMOBIL landscape knows what we're talking about here. Keep an eagle eye out, because a pistol can be sucked up quickly, or a fox cub devoured by the big bad vacuum cleaner.

PLAYMOBIL is economical.
At least, when you calculate over two generations. Based on unconfirmed estimates, one child will have acquired at least 500 Euros worth of PLAYMOBIL by the end of his or her active PLAYMOBIL years. Thanks to the toy's durability, if you store it in a light-proof container, you can pass it on to your own children or grandchildren or auction off your collection at a profit on eBay. Just be sure that the items you want to auction have been absent from the PLAYMOBIL assortment for several years.

PLAYMOBIL creates order.
If you have 500 Euros worth of PLAYMOBIL at home—or even one-fifth of that amount—you understand the importance of a certain minimal degree of order. Tool boxes or sorting containers from a do-it-yourself store or from the Swedish furniture giant can help you sort out weapons, small animals, police equipment and construction tools and to maintain clear order in the PLAYMOBIL chaos for at least a week. Then, at the very latest, you can sort it all out again—at least in the case of two children.

PLAYMOBIL develops patience and dexterity.
Anyone who owns a pirate ship and has ever tried to remove all the cargo that was collected in the storage compartment during a play journey, knows what fine motor skills are all about. Purchasing a grocery store set (item 3200) also requires patience—not to stand in line at the cash register, but to set up and organise the canned foods, bottles and jars. If you want to give one of these large packages as a Christmas or birthday gift (i.e., the knights' castle, modern house or zoo), you should allow yourself at least two hours of assembly time, since—to paraphrase a slogan from the aforementioned Swedish furniture chain—"Are you playing yet, or are you still setting up?"

PLAYMOBIL saves space.
There is room for a PLAYMOBIL dollhouse in even the smallest attic. If the PLAYMOBIL family is taking an adventure cruise on the pirate ship, you can quickly take their house down for the time being. Everything can be disassembled into small, individual pieces, just as it came in the package, and stored compactly. Try that with an expensive wooden dollhouse!

PLAYMOBIL develops concentration.
If, for example, you want to study archaeology later in life, there is nothing better than PLAYMOBIL. A bargain-priced ten litre plastic box filled to the brim with PLAYMOBIL has helped quite a few people delve deeply into their assembly skills. A single motorbike—believe it or not—is made up of 15 individual pieces. If you don't have the instructions, and those pieces are mixed in with 800 pieces from other packages, you can look at this task as a true challenge. With the help of old catalogues, the author of this book spent three very long evenings sorting out the majority of the individual pieces and thereby assembling them into figures, vehicles and accessories in the form in which they were originally produced. Today, she can recognise the upper curve of an exhaust pipe immediately. Thanks to the different colours, she can even tell whether it belongs to an old police motorbike, a chopper or a dirt bike.

Life-sized PLAYMOBIL to get your hands on

PLAYMOBIL Land is a real place: It covers an area of 1 million square feet in the mid-Franconian town of Zirndorf and is heavily guarded. Anyone who wants to enter the "Land of Smiles"—officially known as the PLAYMOBIL FunPark—must first cross a drawbridge, get over the crocodile-filled moat and pass by the armed castle guards. But so far, they have never turned away anyone who was willing to contribute a small fee.

PLAYMOBIL life size

At the FunPark, the familiar PLAYMOBIL world awaits fans large and small in an oversized format. Here, you can board the ship and be a PLAYMOBIL pirate yourself or take your place next to the king's throne as one of the knights. Even the real king of PLAYMOBIL Land, Horst Brandstätter, visits his "playful subjects" from time to time.

Once you're inside, you have the chance of a lifetime to be just like a real little PLAYMOBIL person and do everything that the little figures in the playroom get to do all the time: Storm a knights' castle, venture through the jungle or board the pirate ship (enlarged here from its 23-inch long playroom size to a whopping 56 feet). You can do all of this at the PLAYMOBIL FunPark in Zirndorf, directly adjacent to the geobra Brandstätter company headquarters. Since the year 2000, the PLAYMOBIL world has existed here in size XXL. Inside two pavilions, children can play with all the PLAYMOBIL they ever dreamed of. And next door in the shop, they can try to convince Daddy and Mummy that they need to take all of it home with them. But difficult as it may be to leave the FunPark without purchasing a package, this is not the main idea behind the facility.

PLAYMOBIL life size

The original and the imitation: The farm (item 3072) entered shops in 1999; four years later, a life-size version appeared at the FunPark. Only the milkable cow gave out under the first onrush of fans.

Horst Brandstätter has already invested approximately 30 million Euros here, and the new all-weather event centre cost an additional 50 million Euros. "I want to give my customers, the children, something in return for their loyalty," says the PLAYMOBIL boss. And since stimulating children's imaginations has always been important to him, active play is a subject close to his heart. The rule of the FunPark is quite clearly, "Do it yourself". The FunPark functions without a single fairground ride. The people who come here have to move on their own power. You can pull yourself along on a rope with the ferry boat, run races on little tractors or push little water vehicles through the canal. Likewise, the giant sand and mud area awaits the muscle power of big PLAYMOBIL construction workers. After all, this is just how it is with PLAYMOBIL toys, where—with the exception of the train and the remote controlled vehicles—everything has to be played with by hand. And at every attraction, children prove that they enjoy the active participation. The farm—whose appearance is amaz-

129

PLAYMOBIL life size

The residents of PLAYMOBIL Land point the way through the Land of Smiled. In case of bad weather, there is plenty to do at the indoor dining and event centre.

ingly similar to that of package No. 3072 – was introduced in the summer of 2003. Here, you can milk the cow and give it a drink while myriad other farm animals cavort around you.

Horst Brandstätter himself has contributed many ideas to the park. Since, in addition to his little figures, he especially loves playing golf, the park also includes a 132-yard driving range with 20 teeing grounds and a 3-hole short course with extra large holes. Trainers are on hand to provide advice and help and loan out golf clubs and balls. And in order to ensure that visitors can also enjoy the FunPark in the wintertime or in rainy weather, a gigantic glass house was opened here in October 2005. On five levels, covering an area of 56,000 sq. ft., there is plenty of room for lots and lots of PLAYMOBIL, numerous playground areas, an indoor climbing garden and a dining and entertainment centre.

SLEEPING IN PLAYMOBIL LAND

If you want to stay at PLAYMOBIL Land for several days in a row, you can spend the night at the apart-hotel directly across the road. The facility has rightfully earned the distinction "family friendly". The 422-sq. ft. suites include a living area with parents' bed, along with children's bunk beds in an extra small room. Depending upon the floor, firefighters, airport, Vikings or farm motifs guarantee visitors of colourful PLAY-MOBIL dreams. Incidentally, PLAYMOBIL's head of development, Bernhard Hane, is also responsible for the interior design of the hotel. The PLAYMOBIL Inn looks just the way children (and parents) would want it to: wallpaper decorated with the world-famous face, colourful carpeting, pictures by PLAYMOBIL painter Men Rabe on the walls, and—of course—a little PLAYMOBIL figure as a bedtime treat on the children's pillows. The toothbrush cups featuring the well-known face are expressly intended as souvenirs to be taken home.

In this way, the management is probably hoping that at least the PLAYMOBIL towels will remain at the hotel. Each room contains a refrigerator and a microwave and you can borrow a set of dishes at the hotel reception desk for a deposit, but at no cost. And if all that PLAYMOBIL has put you in the mood to play, you can borrow a box of toys as well: Children can choose between vehicles and farm sets to pass the time until the FunPark opens its gates again at 9:00 the next morning. Up to 10,000 visitors come to the park on a heavy day; spread over a whole year, they number around 700,000, and the PLAYMOBIL Inn is frequently booked to capacity.

After a long day at the FunPark, the PLAYMOBIL Inn invites parents and children to spend a restful night—accompanied, of course, by plenty of PLAYMOBIL accessories.

FUNPARKS WORLDWIDE

You can find FunParks in the locations where PLAYMOBIL is manufactured (Zirndorf and Malta), where the company has its own distribution firms (Paris and Athens), or in the place the boss calls home for half of the year, West Palm Beach, Florida. Horst Brandstätter spends the winter months here, observing the American market and playing golf. In order to stay close to the consumers, he founded the first American FunPark here. A second one is located in the large Florida Mall in Orlando. Unlike the German FunPark, nearly all of the international branches are limited to an indoor area, where there are plenty of opportunities to play with PLAYMOBIL, but no large attractions. The FunPark on Malta includes a small outdoor area with a waterway and a rest area for parents. By now, the FunPark in Zirndorf has become so popular that geobra is currently working on a concept for building and operating additional FunParks within Germany.

In PLAYMOBIL's native town of Zirndorf, the little figures even adorn a fountain.

PLAYMOBIL: A MUSEUM PIECE AND CAST IN BRONZE

However, PLAYMOBIL cannot only be found in playrooms and FunParks. For some time already, the little figures have become museum pieces. Not only do they inspire many modern artists as a motif for paintings, installations or photographs, but there have also been entire exhibitions devoted to the figures and their little world. The first of these was the anniversary exhibit Winzige Weltmacht (Tiny World Power), which appeared in the Nuremberg Toy Museum in 1999 on the occasion of PLAYMOBIL's 25th birthday. Almost simultaneously, the German Toy Museum in Sonnenberg held an exhibit entitled Die Welt im Kinderzimmer (The World in the Playroom). At the time of the toy's 30th birthday, the Historical Museum of the Palatinate presented the nearly six-month long exhibition, PLAYMOBIL—Entdecke die Welt (Discover the World). Afterwards, the exhibits were displayed at the City Museum of Zirndorf and later as a permanent installation at the company's own museum. In Zirndorf, the city of PLAYMOBIL's birth, geobra Brandstätter's success story has already been honoured twice in the City Museum. And along with other toys manufactured in Zirndorf, several bronze PLAYMOBIL figures decorate a city fountain. Unfortunately, a few of these have already lost their heads, since such genuine bronze PLAYMOBIL pieces are quite sought after by collectors.

PLAYMOBIL has been museum material for some time already, since the easy-to-handle little figures have become part of Germany's cultural heritage. Not surprisingly, occasions are constantly being found to put their history and variety on display.

PLAYMOBIL life size

From the first knights to police officers in action, the anniversary exhibit celebrating PLAYMOBIL's 30th birthday traced the development of the world-famous German toy brand.

Caution! PLAYMOBIL can be addictive

They call themselves Hannibal Lecktor (sic), Klicky-Town or Rudewideg, and almost all of them share the same dream —that of finding the ultimate first PLAYMOBIL figure in undamaged packaging, never having been played with. Collecting is a passion—whether the object is Cracker Jack prizes, bar coasters, wristwatches, toy Santa Clauses, egg cups or owls. Nowadays, this starts in school with trendy items such as Pokemon or sports cards and ends in old age with valuable coin collections. The reason why people want to possess as many of a certain thing as possible is difficult to explain.

The passion of collectors

Norway's Erik Skaarup, shown here with Hans Beck, is considered the world's most extensive collector of PLAYMOBIL. He now owns more figures than there are inhabitants in his home town of Kragero: well over 5,000.

Toys have always been a favourite collectors' item, perhaps because so many happy childhood memories are associated with them—or perhaps because the collector never had the object as a child and can now finally fulfil his or her wishes. Dolls, tin soldiers, penny banks and model ships were already being collected 100 years ago. Today's collectors will pay four to five-digit prices at auction for Steiff Teddy bears, old Barbies or model-building kits. PLAYMOBIL also has its collectors. The community is still relatively small, and the passion is a comparatively inexpensive one. Bargains can be found regularly at flea markets or among old toy store inventories. But even here, one collector may pay another as much as 400 Euros for a special package with seven Klickys (collectors' term for the first generation of figures, whose hands were not yet movable). Real added value can also be found in packages which cost an impressive 40 Marks in shops 16 years ago: They can be sold today for around 65 Euros—more than three times the original price. What counts is that the original packaging is intact and none of the individual pieces are missing.

PLAYMOBIL collectors can be divided into two categories: those who play with it, and those who collect it for the sake of owning a complete assortment and who keep the unopened packages sitting on a shelf. "Nobody—with a few exceptions—would buy the entire assortment for their children," says Hans Beck. But such exceptions do exist. One example is Erik Skaarup, a Norwegian pastry chef, who bakes and sells enough cakes to purchase everything made by PLAYMOBIL. Another is Uwe, a 48-year-old advertising display artist who became a "PLAYMOBIL hunter and gatherer" more than ten years ago and who dreams of opening his own PLAYMOBIL museum in Worpswede in Lower Saxony. The fascination is either carried over from the collector's own childhood, or—if he or she was already too old at the time of the 1974 market launch—it is stoked by his or her own children.

A solid core of the collectors' community is already well known in Zirndorf—if only due to their frequent requests for old items or replacement parts—and they met informally for the first time at the FunPark in 2003. Shortly afterward, the first collectors' market was finally held in Herne. Twenty exhibitors from Germany and Austria put their old treasures up for sale, and 90 visitors actually found their way to the city's event centre. PLAYMOBIL fans from the neighbouring Netherlands even dropped by. At the first market, at least, the exhibitors were their own best customers. They happily spent their profits immediately on other old packages. Among the true collectors, actual product exchanges may even take place. If you don't have anything to trade, you can search flea markets or old toy stores for dusty, outdated items—or look on eBay. On any given Friday, 7,368 PLAYMOBIL-related items may be listed for sale at www.ebay.de. Ostensibly, one might think this would be bad for geobra Brandstätter's business. But in fact, the opposite is true. If the quality of the toys is good enough that they can be successfully sold after being stored in the attic for 15 years, parents are happy to fulfil their children's wishes—even if they don't appear to be so cheap at first glance. Parents and collectors bid on eBay in equal numbers; the latter, however, most often on the items that are offered with their original packaging. Once you've been seized by PLAYMOBIL fever, you can easily spend 1,000 Euros per year on your hobby. And watch out—it's very contagious...

A DREAM HOUSE FOR 2,500 EUROS

Gudula Osterhoff displays her version of the "1900" townhouse, not for sale, but simply for everyone's viewing pleasure. Now 26, she began dreaming of her house at the age of 13, when the PLAYMOBIL 1900 series first came on the market. Her parents thought that she was already too old for it. She grew even older, but the dream remained. "And at one point, I stumbled across a fully furnished house at a flea market. That's how it all began," explains the proud homeowner. "But that wasn't enough for me." PLAYMOBIL offers too many nice things, and not all of them will fit into a single house. So she bought a second one, as well as the add-on floors, and eventually began to completely rebuild and widen the house. In her version, the market stands became a shop. For the display windows, her boyfriend used a fine saw to cut out the frames originally intended for a winter garden. But Gudula still had many more ideas. A couple is getting married on the second floor: She assembled the priest needed for the ceremony herself. One flight up, a musician and a painter share an apartment. The latter is in his studio painting a mermaid who is sitting as his model—she's by PLAYMOBIL, of course. In the attic, the children are rummaging in old boxes and trunks, while male and female chimney-sweeps are doing their work on the roof. The Gutersloh native has been collecting since 2001; in that time, she has invested about 2,500 Euros into her hobby. She has decorated each floor individually with dollhouse wallpaper and handmade curtains. The piece stands on a display table in her home. "But not right in front of the window; otherwise it will fade." The only disadvantage: "It is a lot of work to keep it dusted." She never enjoyed playing with the handmade dollhouse that she had as a child—she always wished for one from PLAYMOBIL. "The great thing here is that you can combine everything. Not just all the packages from the pink series, but pieces from other packages as well." Thus, for example, the safe that recently appeared in the police series stands in the stairwell here, being emptied by two robbers who originally appeared as Special figures. Painters have set up scaffolding along the house's facade, and the stretched bearskin from the Viking series serves as a bedside rug. In other words, all is in the true spirit of PLAYMOBIL: Because one thing fits with another.

Just as in real life, the big disadvantage to Gudula Osterhoff's dream house is that you always have to dust. Nevertheless, the purchase price was quite a bit lower than a real house, and she can choose her tenants herself.

The passion of collectors

5,400 LITTLE MEN IN NEAT AND TIDY BOXES

Its inner life is hidden in its hollow head: This is where Martin Cierjacks stores his officers' passports. Here, he records the figure's character traits, strengths and "lineage"—like that of the little red and black man in the picture. When they are not attending collectors' conventions, however, they usually rest neatly in handmade plywood boxes.

Dr. Martin Cierjacks is a trained psychologist, 38 years old and the owner of 5,400 PLAYMOBIL figures. They are divided neatly between a red nation and a green one and now stored in handmade, felt-lined plywood boxes. When you open the lid, a company of soldiers and their officer stands in front of you with military accuracy. Messing everything up with the sweep of her little hand is 14-month-old daughter Fanny's favourite pastime at the moment. But this is something that only she is allowed to do, and which actually ought to bother the doctor, since he sees his collection as "a little piece of order in the world". In his own unique world, that is—which he began building at the age of 12, together with his friend Markus Kolb. The boys had just put their PLAYMOBIL into storage, since they had grown too old for it. "Then PLAYMOBIL brought out the pirate series, and my best friend and I briefly regretted that we were already past the recommended age for it. Nevertheless, we each bought one pirate and rearranged the pieces to create individual noblemen," says the Mannheim native, remembering the project's harmless beginnings. "Proud of our creations, we got together to play, until he had one more soldier, who arrested my nobleman. The next time I had two soldiers and he had five; there were battles, and other people joined in." For thirteen years, he shared this unusual passion with a total of three friends. The nations traded with each other, kidnapped important figures and fought battles. When everyone's collections became too large, and simply setting up the companies would have taken hours, PLAYMOBIL ambassadors stepped in to work out deals. The stories filled entire history books, and all the participants recorded the events fastidiously after each meeting. Whether or not the others are still collecting is unknown. But at least in the case of Martin Cierjacks, the fascination still remains; he continues to expand his nations to this day. He purchases the small parts that he needs through dealers who are familiar with him and his special collection. "None of my figures was ever available at PLAYMOBIL in its current form." As a holdover from the games with his friends, their identification papers are still inside their heads. Each nobleman or head of state has an individual passport hidden under his wig. In tiny, neat lettering, the paper records which group the figure belongs to—the "red and dark grey people", for example. Points are awarded for strengths and talents based on an elaborate system; but general character traits are also an essential element. When asked what he finds so appealing about collecting PLAYMOBIL, he pauses for a moment: "Maybe it's the colour and shape of the figures. Maybe it's the similarity with reality, which nevertheless remains abstract. Maybe it's the sound that the little men make when you put them together, when the head snaps back onto the torso."

THE PLAYMOBIL OPERA

Daniela Schabenstiel can also call an entire population of PLAYMOBIL people her own. They have appeared in various displays, but are currently on their way to the opera. For almost four years, she has been building a large city opera house, which bears a strong resemblance to the one found in Vienna. "The idea of building an opera house out of PLAYMOBIL came to me more or less in the first moment that I saw the pink 'fairy tale castle'," the 36-year-old Daniela remembers. However, she had already been a collector for quite some time. What entered her room as just a normal toy when she was seven years old has remained with her to this day. "As a child, first of all, I had knights, the circus, the farm with lots of horses, the zoo, the hospital and the pirates. But for each of these, I had the complete set with all of the accessories. Today, with just a few exceptions, I have almost everything PLAYMOBIL has ever made." By now, the toys fill 60 moving boxes. Whatever she needs for a given scenario, she assembles into large dioramas. This was also little Daniela's favourite thing to do. "Just as they do now, the dioramas told little stories. The larger the scene, the more individual stories there are to discover. In the knights' tournament, I always re-enacted the scene from 'Ivanhoe', for example where Ivanhoe chooses his lady from the audience by presenting her with a tiara on the end of his lance."

But to get back to the current display: The adult Daniela has always been fascinated by opera. In order to hear Plácido Domingo, she travels by train for nights at a time all over Germany so as not to miss any of his performances. At home as she is in the opera houses of Europe, it is no wonder that at first glance, she associated the PLAYMOBIL-style chandeliers and balconies not with a castle but with an opera house. From here, she very slowly developed the idea of building a "real" opera house, with everything that that entails: dressing rooms, tailor shop, equipment area, property room, make-up rooms, set painters, canteen, ballet studio and artistic directors' office. "Over the past years, of course, it has taken on a life of its own. The original plan to build a small theatre has evolved into a gigantic complex. To the point where my husband insisted that the men in the audience be properly attired; that precipitated a large order for little men in black suits," the "architect" laughs. The opera house is also a new challenge because, "I've never done a major construction of this kind before". Incidentally, her medieval framework city now consists of 20 houses, some of which never existed at PLAYMOBIL—for example, a cathedral, a school, a hospital, and, of course, a pharmacy, because in addition to pursuing her PLAYMOBIL passion, Daniela Schabenstiel works as a pharmaceutical technical assistant.

Three children, three PLAYMOBIL countries: "Marionien", "Schlummerland" and "Wunibaldinien" are the three imaginary nations invented by the three Czaika children. They stand in the basement of their parents' home to this day and are still played with regularly. Of course, the PLAYMOBIL fans were sometimes laughed at, but they also received a great deal of admiration from their classmates. "And if we sometimes didn't really want to admit to it, we would describe it as a model train with a surrounding landscape."

THREE SIBLINGS—ONE PASSION

Their names are Irmtraud, Otfried and Ingrid; they are 39, 32 and 25 years old, and their PLAYMOBIL world is thought to be the largest assembled PLAYMOBIL collection in Germany. In three basement rooms of their parents' house in Füssen, over a space of 450 sq. ft., you can admire everything that Hans Beck and his successors have come up with—but not simply in the form in which the toys appeared on the market at the time, but rather, combined together to form entire medieval cities, various kings' courts and Western streets. Whatever was not available in the PLAYMOBIL assortment, the siblings initially made by hand out of wood or cardboard; later, they rebuilt the sections using PLAYMOBIL walls and individual parts. The correspondence between the siblings and PLAYMOBIL already fills and entire ring binder. Along with page-long order lists for hundreds of individual parts, they commented on every new product, wrote postcards from holidays and sent little photo albums. Today, the contents of the basement rooms are equal in value to a small car. But in fact, it all started very harmlessly in the mid-1970s. Otfried, then four years old, received a PLAYMOBIL firefighter as a small gift from an acquaintance. Some time later, this was joined by a washerwoman, courtesy of older sister Irmtraud. "Then it came to a halt: Our parents were against this new system, since we were already committed to the LEGO system through our eldest sis-

ter (now 42). Nevertheless, one year later, our grandparents gave us a drugstore. Then we added cowboys, Indians, knights, other figures and old city buildings." When the family moved to a larger house, the children were given their own PLAYMOBIL room in the attic. All of their pocket money and extra earnings were channelled into the little plastic world. Both sisters—whether seven years older or seven years younger—shared the hobby. "Finally, we had so many PLAYMOBIL buildings that each of the three of us could build a little castle. We founded three kingdoms: Marionien, Schlummerland and Wunibaldinien." The castles turned into fortresses, and the kingdoms ended in a revolution. "The internal tension of trying to unify knights, contemporary figures and Indians as well as Eskimos, Arabs and cowboys was the downfall of these kingdoms. Today they all live peacefully side-by-side on a fictitious continent. The knights have a kingdom; their King Olav resides at Adlerhorst Castle. The rest of the people live in the Free Republic of Flachland, a nation with its own constitution, a president, and lots of small-minded but loveable citizens. The railway system converges in the capital city of Halwö."
However, the siblings grew older, and little by little, they left their PLAYMOBIL paradise. Elder sister Irmtraud was the first to move out, taking her portion with her. She now has three children of her own, and her husband is a building contractor, who gladly let himself be infected. As an advertising strategy for his building company, he rented a large display window in Marktoberdorf, where new PLAYMOBIL worlds appear every three to four months. Whether it's Villa Villekulla, Formula 1 racing, a beach promenade with hotel and camping area or the building of the pyramids—he comes up with the ideas and Irmtraud figures out how to execute them, orders the individual pieces and assembles the scene. Every other weekend, she drives to Füssen with her children and plays in the PLAYMOBIL basement. Ingrid, the music student, also returns every week. The brother ended up in faraway Stockholm; he drops by only occasionally. Nevertheless, his new house contains—quite fittingly for his expatriate home in Sweden—a complete Viking world and a large airport facility. Perhaps he is a bit homesick for his PLAYMOBIL Land…

True PLAYMOBIL fans waited for Egyptian and Roman series for a long time. In their own rented display window, Irmtraud Czaika advertises her husband's building company with the help of ever-changing PLAYMOBIL worlds.

A FANTASY-FILLED CHILDHOOD WITH PLAYMOBIL

Oliver Schaffer is a musical theatre performer from Hamburg. His dream of appearing on the world's stages was strongly influenced by PLAYMOBIL. In 1981, a colourful package filled with little figures appeared under the Christmas tree for the first time, and he was immediately enthralled. This fascination—along with his growing interest in circuses and show business—made him into a passionate PLAYMOBIL collector. His parents supported him at first; later, his pocket money had to suffer for his addiction. He quickly acquired everything that could be even remotely useful for his circus show. He didn't hide his passion from his classmates, either—but they could only shrug their shoulders when Oliver preferred to work on a new circus programme rather than playing with them.
With PLAYMOBIL's help, he brought his "Circus Oliver" to life. His father helped him build a big top and animal stables out of wood and canvas; his mother designed the hand-printed programmes on the typewriter, with such melodious names as "Dreams and Illusion" and "Exotica". Over the years, he perfected his circus world, and his own room quickly became too small. The PLAYMOBIL performers replayed acts from well known circuses such as Roncalli, Circus Krone and Barum. Lighting equipment, loudspeakers

and real sawdust were added; in the outdoor circus "Oliver Romani", wolves performed new dressage acts. Finally, Oliver even added an amusement park with a small railroad, parades and various thematic areas.
The 16x16-foot world, complete with railroad connection, vehicle fleet and open air stage, now rests neatly packed in his parents' attic. His dream of sharing his PLAYMOBIL past with other people—especially children—has been fulfilled since 2003, when his model circus was displayed to the public as part of the anniversary exhibition.

The passion of collectors

PLAYMOBIL ALLOWS SO MUCH ROOM FOR CREATIVITY

Oliver Deeg, now 31, is a true PLAYMOBIL child. Early on, kind relatives gave him a city guard room, a prison tower, a city hall and a bakery. "This way, the PLAYMOBIL community could govern, feed and defend itself (later on, even against pirates…). Besides everything having to do with knights and pirates, my first favourite contemporary set was the double-decker plane. I kept it with me almost all the time, and I liked to fly around our garden with it." In addition to the toys themselves, the Freiburg native was fascinated by the hairstyles. "I still remember that as a little boy, I showed my barber a little PLAYMOBIL man and demanded that he cut my hair in the same style—unfortunately he refused." Following a ten year break from PLAYMOBIL, he started collecting at the age of 24. "While I was writing my degree dissertation, I bought myself a dragon as a little mascot and set it on top of my PC monitor." The dragon eventually evolved into an entire fantasy knights' world in the style of The Lord of the Rings. "I converted this into a photo story on my Internet site, www.playfans.com, with the title Das Schwert der Macht (The Sword of Power)". To this end, he has since added the following to his collection: nine pirate ships (large, small, new and old), three old space stations, two large knights' castles, one small knights' castle, two dragon's temples, two baron's battle towers, all of the American knight action sets, (unfortunately) just one white half-timbered farmhouse, the old train station, five jet airliners, everything from the new Viking series, everything from the jungle series, various space sets, 20 vampires…

Naturally, he also creates his own figures, new buildings and vehicles: "Using the three small pirate ships, I built six new variations by recombining the same pieces." In addition to surfing on eBay, visiting flea markets and chasing after remainder stock, the drumming teacher enjoys trading with like-minded collectors—for example, on his last trip to the USA, where he met with the "Play-fans" he'd gotten to know online. "I've developed some real friendships, which I'd no longer want to be without!"

What he can't find in Zirndorf, the real fan builds himself: Kurt Cobain of Nirvana, German pop singer Heino and comedian Stefan Raab are Oliver Deeg's own creations.

The passion of collectors

KLICKY WAS ON THE INTERNET

The "Playmosketeers" are a small group of PLAYMOBIL fans who maintain their own PLAYMOBIL websites about their hobby, and who met on the Internet about eight years ago. The founding father of the "Playmosketeers" and of the entire online fan community is Richard Silvano, age 67, a psychologist and management consultant from Fort Lauderdale, Florida. He was the first to launch his PLAYMOBIL fan website more than nine years ago, and he brought the "Playmosketeers" together via daily e-mail exchanges.

At that time, the Internet was practically a blank slate as far as the subject of PLAYMOBIL was concerned. Any topics or information beyond the "official" PLAYMOBIL website were almost non-existent; there was only a small handful of websites for PLAYMOBIL fans. The two most important of these were probably Richard Silvano's Internet site, www.gardenwargaming.com—containing tips and tricks for any "PLAYMOBIL crafters" who want to make their own figures and accessories—and the site created by Bart De Smet of Belgium, www.playmobilcentral.de. This was a giant catalogue, aimed especially at collectors, which not only depicted the current PLAYMOBIL product line, but, more importantly, contained essential information and photos of old and rare PLAYMOBIL products. The information on this private collectors' site was presented so well that Internet users believed they were on the official PLAYMOBIL website—which the name playmobilcentral could also lead one to believe. The people in Zirndorf were not very happy with the situation, and successfully sued for the fan site to be disconnected in order to protect their rights to the trademark. The Internet PLAYMOBIL fan community, in turn, was very angry, and mobilised themselves—very much in the style of the musketeers, "all for one and one for all"—against PLAYMOBIL with a friendly but massive e-mail campaign. This event was known as the "Klicky War", and the fans quickly made their voices heard. Finally, the two sides agreed on clear guidelines as to what should and should not be allowed on a private PLAYMOBIL Internet site, and Bart De Smet's site was allowed back on the Net using the new address, www.collectobil.com. Today, Bart De Smet is officially employed by PLAYMOBIL Belgium, developing games and other features for the firm's own PLAYMOBIL website.

Other important Internet sites:
www.bollian.de
www.claudia-schott.de

A LITTLE COLLECTORS' GLOSSARY:

 For a PLAYMOBIL collector, "customising" refers to the technique—probably first developed in the USA—of dismantling each PLAYMOBIL figure into its individual parts with the help of a vice and a screwdriver and rebuilding it according to one's own tastes, or to the creation of home-made accessories using special plastic craft materials.

 In the so-called "Hans Beck method", the figure is cracked open while its legs are bent, in order to extract the head from the "skeleton".

 Collectors use the following terms to describe the condition of a given PLAYMOBIL item (these terms, by the way, apply to all other areas of collecting as well):

- MIB means Mint (brand new, untainted, flawless) in Box—that is, in the package and not played with.
- Near Mint refers to a product which has been played with gently or a box which has slight storage damage.
- A collector's greatest joy is a NRFB PLAYMOBIL package—that is, "never removed from box"; in other words, exactly as PLAYMOBIL delivered it.
- Particularly high bids are placed on special edition products or international packages produced by licensing companies who manufactured PLAYMOBIL on behalf of geobra Brandstätter—such as the Greek firm Lyra, the Antex Andina company from Argentina, Spain's Famobil, Schaper from the USA, Brazil's Trol/Estela or England's Marx.

The passion of collectors

Goldwater Creek is located in the middle of Dortmund, Germany. If that's too far to travel, you can follow the events in the Wild West at www.playmotown.de.

SHOWDOWN IN GOLDWATER CREEK

Sven Hanning is a purist. Even as a child, he wanted only pure PLAYMOBIL, not to be combined with any other toys. The only exception was the "gold nuggets" that he made himself for his gold mine, since the Wild West theme fascinated the now 24-year-old Sven most of all. Between the ages of three and eleven, he actively played with PLAYMOBIL, either alone or with his older brother. Even later on, he did not lose interest in the toy, but continued to follow all of the new products. He thought, "One day when I have enough money, I want to make some of my dreams come true." But when he noticed that more and more products were being removed from the assortment, he decided he had better act immediately. "Shortly before Christmas 2001, when I saw an incredibly inexpensive offer for a combination of the castle defenders and the siege tower, I bought PLAYMOBIL again for the first time since my childhood. And after that, I didn't stop..." The medieval diorama that he built has long since given way to his Wild West town, "Goldwater Creek". Here, Sheriff William 'Playmo-Bill' Widowman, Doc Swanberg, Nevada Bob, teacher Katie Lang and undertaker Mr. Fu, live out exciting adventures which Sven meticulously photographs, subtitles and displays on the Internet. Now every PLAYMOBIL fan can enjoy the comics created by the psychology student from Dortmund. To find out what happens next in Goldwater Creek, log on to www.playmotown.de. It's worth a click...

After more than 30 years of PLAYMOBIL, someone finally made the effort to document every product that PLAYMOBIL has ever made. Here, collectors can indulge their passion with over 2,000 photographs. The book not only depicts all of the figures and sets that PLAYMOBIL has manufactured up until the present day, but it also shows such details as the various types of packaging used for the same articles and sets which were (or are) only available in other countries. Incidentally, the author, Axel Hennel, also collects PLAYMOBIL, but only items from its first year, 1974.

The passion of collectors

Puzzle 24

playmobil

All around the playroom,
or all the places you can put a PLAYMOBIL logo

PLAYMOBIL—by now it is much more than just a 2.9-inch tall figure. The world-famous face is showing up on more and more items which—according to market researchers—children can also use in their playrooms. Merchandising is the concept of getting even more profit out of a good idea. Nevertheless, the people in Zirndorf are quite careful about allocating licenses. Even though the little figures' friendly smiles have appeared on a wide range of products—from wallpaper to shoes to bedding—over the course of three decades, the toy itself continues to be the most important thing.

More than a figure

PLAYMOBIL sells well. This logically leads one to consider using it to help market other products. Just two years after the product launch, PLAYMOBIL fretwork sets appeared on the market. You could choose between twelve different scenes from the lives of the little construction workers, travellers, knights, firefighters, cowboys and police officers, at different levels of difficulty and in four sizes. "First cut, then paint", was the slogan. A PLAYMOBIL theatre book entitled In the Wild West was released in 1977. The book contained two actual theatre sets in which children could play with PLAYMOBIL figures. The story texts were printed on the side walls. These items were followed by colouring books, puzzles, a sticker game, card games, records, a lotto game and comic books. Yes, you could even decorate children's rooms with wallpaper depicting colourful farm or construction site scenes. At that time, all of these items were still marketed by PLAYMOBIL Merchandising GmbH. One particularly original idea was a thermometer, which children could first paint and then hang on the window.

148

Attempts at PLAYMOBIL clothing, primarily sweatshirts, shirts and pyjamas—even manufactured by such well-known labels as Schiesser—were abandoned after a short time. Other licensed products included WMF children's flatware, plates, cups, pitchers and egg cups printed with PLAYMOBIL figures and vehicles.

In the late 1990s, the first children's eyewear collection was introduced, including matching glasses cases. By 2004, the fourth collection was already on the market. A fire engine alarm clock was developed with a flashing light and a realistic-sounding approaching siren to call children to duty in the morning. Even PLAYMOBIL wristwatches are available. Stickers and notebook labels herald the start of the school term; matching "Schultüten" (traditional German cardboard cones filled with candy, which children receive on the first day of first grade) appeared beginning in 2002. This was not actually a new invention: A PLAYMOBIL "Schultüte" had been produced once before—not for filling with candy yourself, but already outfitted with a PLAYMOBIL school class, schedule and notebook labels.

More than a figure

SWEET ON THE OUTSIDE— PLAYMOBIL ON THE INSIDE

The French especially (who, after the Germans, are the most PLAYMOBIL-crazed nation) like things sweet. Just in time for Easter, business booms with all kinds of surprise eggs: sweet on the outside, with toys on the inside. In 1999, the Carrefour trade chain offered a variation with an inner PLAYMOBIL figure in their stores to great success. The Japanese love sweets as well. Here, PLAYMOBIL took advantage of people's cravings and attempted to make themselves known to Japanese children by way of cookies. In 1982, each cookie package from Japan's Meiji biscuit factory contained a PLAYMOBIL figure, helping to increase awareness of the product.

Herpa, a specialty model car company from Dietenhofen, offers big PLAYMOBIL fans something to dream about. Anyone who hasn't quite saved enough money for the original product can purchase a BMW Z4 in 1:18 scale for the PLAYMOBIL world. A test-driving PLAYMOBIL couple is included. The accurately detailed, sturdy Playcars are available at BMW dealerships or in toy stores.

PLAYMOBIL FOR THE EARS

People quickly realised that the stories you can act out with PLAYMOBIL are also ideally suited to audio recordings. In 1975, ARIOLA released the first long-playing records, The Secret of Burg Klopfstein and Our Sheriff is the Best. Twelve years later, audio cassettes were available from EUROPA. Professor Mobilux and his Irish assistant Patrick F. Patrick experience exciting adventures, discover secrets and impede evil-doers. In order for children to play along while listening, the appropriate figures were available as item 3099—and of course, the professor only travels to worlds which can be built with PLAYMOBIL. Naturally, a matching cassette case with PLAYMOBIL motifs needed to be produced as well. Since 1998, Universal has marketed three cassettes with the themes "Alarm Signal", "Prince Lionheart's Adventure" and "Holidays on the Farm". In the same year, three computer games were introduced as tie-ins to the farm, knight and dollhouse themes. Two years later, children could also take them along to play on their GameBoys. Colouring books for small children, painting sets where kids could paint police motorcycles or knights by the numbers and sticker and picture books accompanied by a PLAYMOBIL figure were other licensed products—all of which are no longer available.

More than a figure

PLAYMOBIL SMILES FROM DUSK TO DAWN

Since 1997, the merchandising agency BAVARIA SONOR has been responsible for PLAYMOBIL's licensing business. It promotes a selected assortment of licensed products which complement the PLAYMOBIL brand: for example, puzzles—ranging from framed puzzles for the smallest children to 100 to 200-piece scenes of knights or pirate ships. The same manufacturer also produces two dice games: Pirate Chase and Knight Run. If you even want to dream about PLAYMOBIL, you can cuddle up in the Viking bedding set and continue playing on the play carpet the next morning. And if you're extra nice to your mother, you might even get a T-shirt embroidered with PLAYMOBIL figures—since a PLAYMOBIL embroidery pattern chip is available for the Bernina sewing machine. A bag collection and a calendar were also introduced in 2004. And then, of course, there are the freebies from the geobra Brandstätter company itself, such as balloons, buttons, FunCards with stickers or tattoos included, key rings or rubber stamps.

Rembrandt, Tischbein and 10,312 PLAYMOBIL figures—
a toy conquers the art world

Playing with PLAYMOBIL is not an art—anyone can do it. But what began as a harmless children's toy has long since become a cult object. And if you look at all the works of art that have been created around the theme of PLAYMOBIL, you might even think it was a genre of its own.

PLAYMOBIL in art

As early as 1976, Professor Robert Gutmann wrestled with the question: "Is the basic figure of the so-called PLAYMOBIL system a recognised work of art?" He pondered this issue at geobra Brandstätter's request in connection with the plagiarism suit brought against the competing product, PlayBIG. He investigated thoroughly and came to this conclusion: "The figure created by Hans Beck should be categorised as a work of art. One should not be distracted by the fact that it is 'only' a little figure and 'only' the prototype for a toy intended for mass production. The single important issue is that this figure became a character by means of its creator's artistic skills."

25 years after Hans Beck's artistic accomplishment, the first PLAYMOBIL generation began occupying itself with this influential object of its childhood. Playart was the name of the exhibition held at the Schwarzenberg gallery in a back courtyard in Berlin, in honour of the toy's 25th birthday. In video installations, photography, pop-art and PLAYMOBIL installations, the artists paid tribute to their one-time favourite toy.

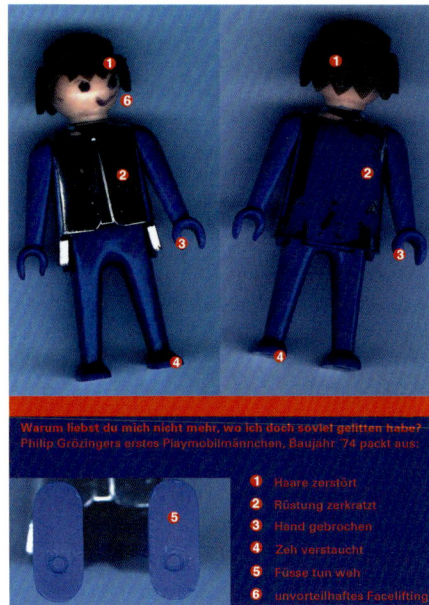

PLAYMOBIL LEAVES ITS MARK—ON ARTISTS AS WELL

Philip Grözinger, curator of the exhibition, immortalised his very first little PLAYMOBIL man in the form of a digital photograph printed on canvas. "It was the winter of 1974, when St. Nicholas brought him the little knight, stuck into his brown fur boot along with the mandarins and gingerbread." (From Playart-Dokumentation.)

"Why don't you love me anymore, when I have suffered so much?" St. Nicholas's now-battered gift asks its owner 25 years later.

In 1999, the first generation of Playmokids was all grown up. What was once a fascination with the toy had become a reflection on societal events. Thanks to its proliferation and its unchanged facial expression—the dot, dot, dash—the PLAYMOBIL figure has long since become a pop art icon. But rather than the smiling face, it was the printed feet that appealed to Sebastian Mayer, a photographer from Berlin. "What would a living PLAYMOBIL figure look like?" or "How has PLAYMOBIL left its mark on me?" might be the questions behind his photo. On the one hand—as the copyright notation on the foot indicates—the PLAYMOBIL figure represents a copiously distributed, industrially manufactured product. On the other hand, it also represents a toy which holds personal memories for almost every person who played with it in his or her childhood, and which has left its stamp on that person. Perhaps someone who, like the foot model in the photo, was also born in 1974.

Previous page: Marek McBanek: Untitled, acrylic on canvas, 58.5 x 66.3 inches.

In the four-part photo series, Glücklicher Wohnen (Live More Happily), Julia Schnitzer projected Playmos onto the London Underground, the Mexican prairie, or—as shown here—the meadows of her homeland.

PLAYMOBIL in art

Left: "Why did you leave me?" asks Philip Grözinger's first PLAYMOBIL figure in the 39 x 54.6 inch high acrylic painting done by the curator himself. It is able to smile again, however, because—25 years after their first meeting—its owner has devoted an entire exhibition to it. To be an object upon which children and adults can project their fantasies constitutes, for Grözinger, "the myth of the PLAYMOBIL figure".

Below: The copyright stamp on real feet characterises Sebastian Mayer's interpretation of the theme.

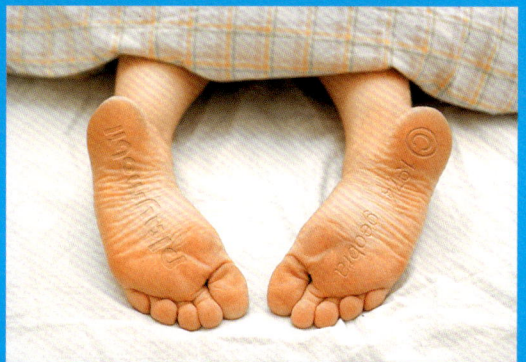

Above: The "playmades" by C.X. Huth appear in their Playland in a similar size (46.8 x 39 inches). The ridges on their heads for clicking on hats, as well as the gripping hands, are easily recognisable. Artistic license takes over only in the case of the arms, since real PLAYMOBIL girls cannot extend their arms to the side.

PLAYMOBIL in art

KEEP SMILING, NO MATTER WHAT HAPPENS

Men Rabe, born in Odenwald in 1946, deals with the PLAYMOBIL figures differently than the members of the PLAYMOBIL generation. In Zirndorf, you can find his paintings everywhere you look. They decorate the rooms of the PLAYMOBIL Hotel; and in the entryway of the company's headquarters hangs his perhaps best-known work, Goethe, an homage to Tischbein's famous painting, Goethe in Italy. Only in his picture, it is not Goethe who travels to Italy, but a "Gesellschaftsattrappe" or "cultural template", as he calls his figures: big eyes, always smiling—just like at PLAYMOBIL. If you look behind the plastic facade, you can see the person, who—like the figure—lives in a world of feigned individuality. Like the materials that surround him, he is reduced to the level of a mass-produced product. Anything negative disappears behind the frozen-on attitude of "keep smiling". Men Rabe paints using classical techniques, and he loves form just as much as he loves embellishing his subjects with precise details, all the way down to the drapery. This explains his fondness for transposing the works of Raphael, Leonardo or Tischbein onto contemporary people.

Be it Goethe or the princess and the frog prince, Men Rabe can imagine any subject using the "cultural templates" of the PLAYMOBIL figures and their eternal smiles.

PLAYMOBIL in art

REMBRANDT PAINTS PLAYMOBIL

Jorge Villalba-Strohecker likes things even more classical. He re-interpreted Rembrandt's Night Watch in a 1:1 ratio of 11.78 feet high by 14.37 feet long, using the original technique. After thoroughly studying the famous painting in Amsterdam's Rijksmuseum, he decorated his PLAYMOBIL figures. He moulded settings and costumes out of polyurethane material and painted them. The faces bore a likeable, ironic expression. After assembling the "live" model, he photographed his composition using the same lighting conditions as in the original. He then used the photo as a master for his oil painting. Jorge Villalba-Strohecker was intrigued by the idea of replacing the baroque characters with lifeless contemporary figures. The observer should recognise the original painting yet be surprised by the presence of PLAYMOBIL figures standing in for the characters. "The PLAYMOBIL figures' unshakeable expression makes the original painting a subject of intentional but friendly irony," Villalba-Strohecker believes.

Original or forgery? Only the protagonists distinguish Jorge Villalba-Strohecker's Night Watch from the original. The size, painting style and lighting are based as closely as possible on the great master's model.

157

MASS PRODUCED PRODUCT OR INDIVIDUAL?

The unwavering smiles and the massive scale of production are the fundamental themes of many artists' examinations of their 2.9 inch-high childhood memory. In 1993, Kiki Ahlers presented her installation, Anita, for the first time in Hamburg. In a 1300 sq. ft. space, she set up 10,312 white PLAYMOBIL figures in a grid-like formation. On the wall behind them, the exact same number of German civil registry office-approved first names was displayed in alphabetical order. Anyone who wished to could purchase the blank figure of his or her choice in a signed and numbered box for 20 Marks. The piece was an allusion to the nearly compulsive practice of imposing

Kiki Ahlers' installation, Anita (below), individualised 10,312 PLAYMOBIL figures by assigning exactly the same number of first names to the meticulously placed little people. Anyone who chose to could purchase his or her "favourite" figure.

PLAYMOBIL in art

Above and left: The World Are Many Slices was a limited-time wall painting by master class pupil Ralf Gemein, who painted it on site in the John-Doe-Kunstraum in Düsseldorf. The work was on view through a display window for four weeks.

Leben-Säule (Pillar of Life) is the title of this 8.2 foot high sculpture by Ingo Klöcker—a room installation which would certainly make some children's hearts beat faster.

identity and identifiableness onto objects by giving them names. Little by little, holes actually did appear in the installation's grid.

Ralf Gemein, an art student and master class pupil at the Düsseldorf Art Academy, showed himself to be equally industrious in November 2001. For six days, he worked for 15 hours a day on his 11.5 x 16.4 foot painting, Die Welt sind viele Scheiben (The World Are Many Slices). The work was not intended to last forever, since the walls of the John-Doe-Kunstraum—which can only be observed through a display window—were repainted one month later. Due to their reduced nature, Ralf Gemein sees the PLAYMOBIL figures more as an anonymous collection of geometric shapes than as figures with personalities and characteristics. It is only the observer who expects there to be a story. And this, in fact, may be the very reason that the paintings are of PLAYMOBIL figures and not of some other object.

IT'S THE QUANTITY THAT COUNTS

Art and design professor Dr. Ingo Klöcker of Fürth makes picture assemblages out of—among other things—PLAYMOBIL. His Stetson is assembled from hundreds of PLAYMOBIL cowboy hats. In works such as Das Ständchen (The Serenade) as well, PLAYMOBIL scenes are frozen into the contents of a mixed-media assemblage. A moment of play is preserved for all time. The works are intended to have an "aha!" effect on the observer, who walks into an exhibit and encounters something very familiar. "Oh, of course we know each other" instead of "What was the artist thinking there?" It is easy to make friends with something familiar.

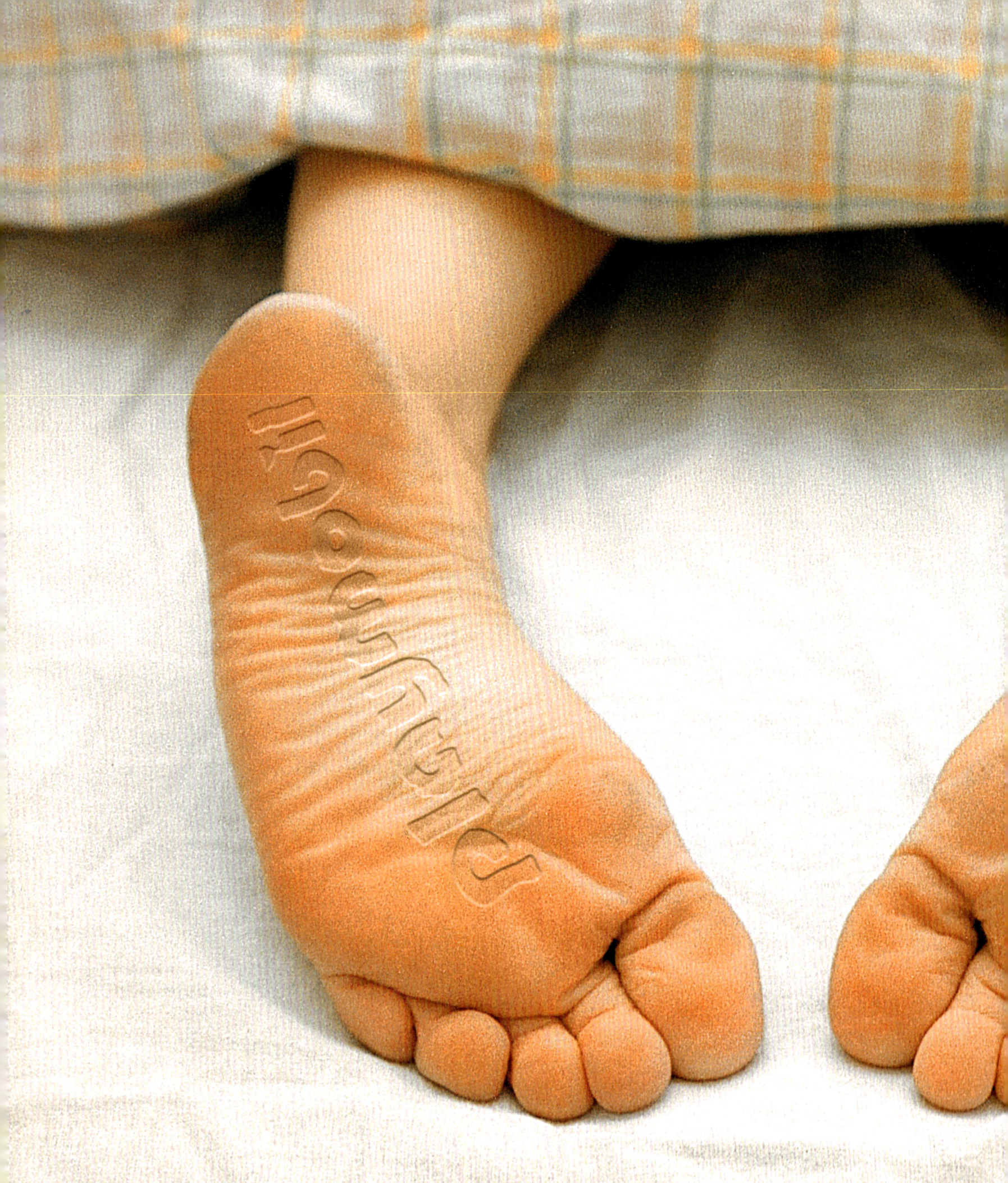

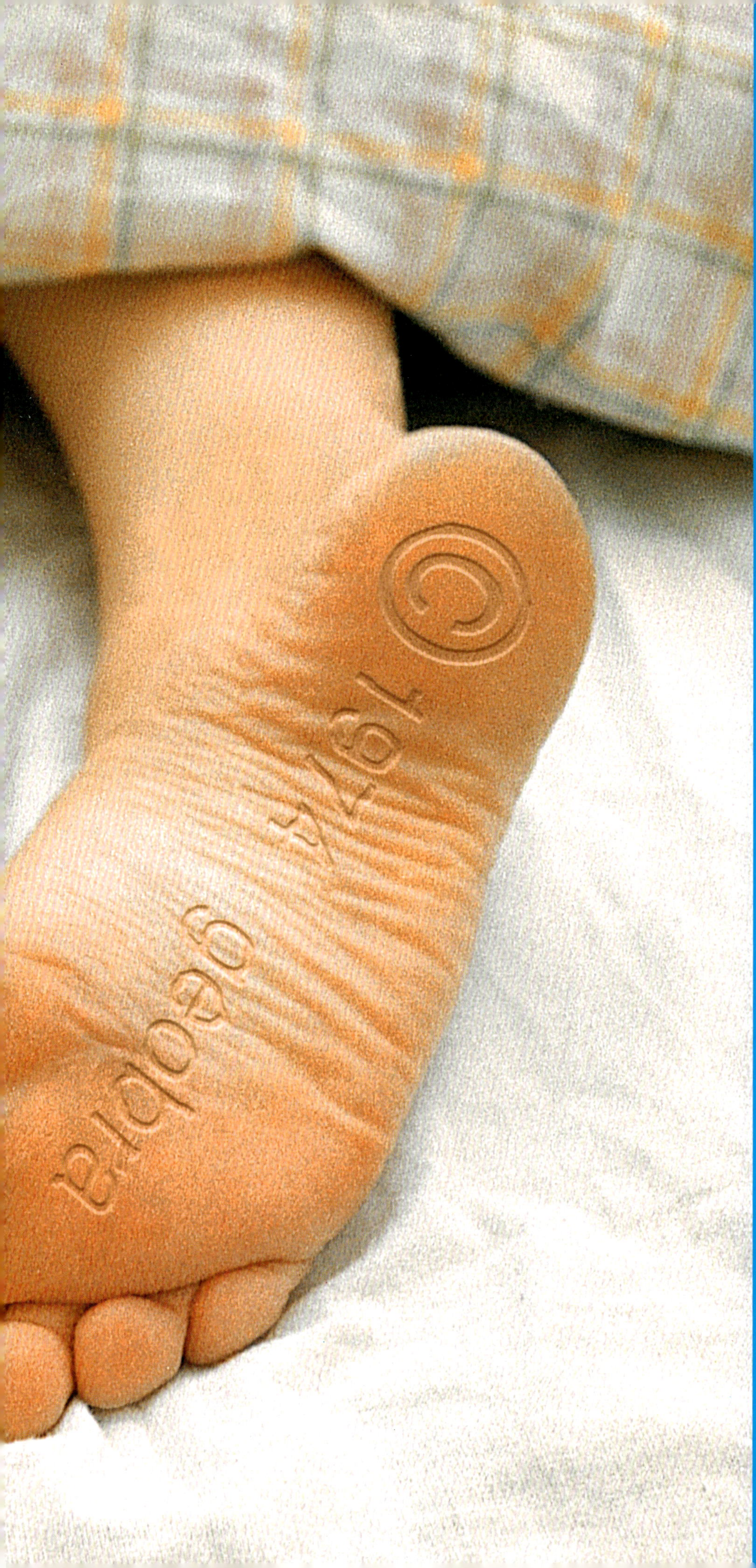

PLAYMOBIL—more than a toy

Over the past 30 years, PLAYMOBIL has become much more than simply a toy for children. Artists examine it, collectors spend large sums of money on it, and the little figures have long since taken their place in our day-to-day culture as a cult object. Whether rebuilt in sand, immortalised in books or used as the subject of photographs—there is hardly anything that hasn't been done with PLAYMOBIL.

...more than a toy

LATE NIGHT SHOW

Late night television host Harald Schmidt used the little products for a long time. On his original talk show, he employed them regularly to create graphic illustrations of subjects in need of explanation. Whether he wanted to depict Franz Kafka's Metamorphosis, Orpheus in the Underworld or the Ring of the Nibelung, his property master and man with the water glass, Sven Schmidt, found the right materials for every topic in the PLAYMOBIL assortment. And Sven Schmidt admitted, "I have more fun playing with PLAYMOBIL now than I did as a kid." At first, the people in Zirndorf were not terribly pleased when even Hitler and Stalin were represented by PLAYMOBIL figures, but with the passage of time, even the Franconians endorsed the night-time educational programme (which, however, appeared on German screens for the last time at Christmas 2003). When, in one of their first television appearances, the little people were still held in place with modelling clay, Horst Brandstätter remembered that the company had also sold stands for them in the early years. The firm began making the little platforms again out of transparent plastic, exclusively for the Harald Schmidt Show.

STICK ONE ON

In 1999, the first PLAYMOBIL postage stamp appeared—ironically enough, in the home country of its biggest competitor, LEGO. Four Colours was the name of the picture, which in art historical terms, belongs to the category of editorial images. The artist Thomas Kluge used four of the first little PLAYMOBIL men to create a photorealistic depiction of the four colours yellow, red, blue and green. Of course, he could also have done this with LEGO blocks; but after all, Denmark has been one of PLAYMOBIL's most successful export markets since 1975.

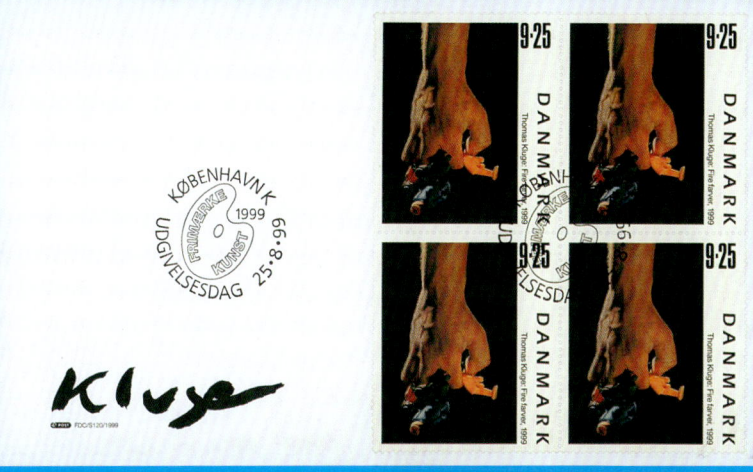

HEALTHY ACTIVITY

Du und Deine Arzneimittel (You and your medications) was the name of this event, co-sponsored in 1983 by pharmacies, the state-run German health insurance company AOK and the Hamburg public health authority. The exhibit illustrated important information about health and medicine, long before today's era of health care reform. In order to demonstrate how food makes its way through the body, the clever Northern Germans created a model of the entire digestive tract, letting PLAYMOBIL figures do the hard work of bacteria and enzymes. Not surprisingly, this portion of the exhibit was the most heavily attended one.

BUILT IN THE SAND

The second Sandworld festival in Travemünde, Germany in 2003 could not do without PLAYMOBIL, either. Unlike in real "life", however, here it was disproportionately large. As the carvers (the professional sand sculpture builders) pointed out, it was constructed in the children's section. As the Sandworld organisers' statement explains, "The reason that a PLAYMOBIL figure was selected was that this is a beloved, internationally recognised toy."

...more than a toy

PLAYMOBIL FOR BEGINNING READERS

In the LesePiraten series produced by the LoeweVerlag in Bindlach, a PLAYMOBIL knight becomes the brave hero. Illustrator Peter Nieländer and author Martin Klein created a real tribute to the PLAYMOBIL knights. Steadfast Jonathan lives through a terrible tale of woe: Carried off by a brutal monster (the cat), abducted by a feathered dragon (a bird) and imprisoned in its lair, and shot into the air by a ruthless giant (with a New Year's Eve firecracker)—he finally lands in his owner's radish garden, quite the worse for wear. Although the word PLAYMOBIL never appears, the order of knights to which the steadfast Jonathan belongs is clear from the first illustration.

THE RED HOUSE

A simple decorating trick has kept PLAYMOBIL collectors scrambling for years, searching in vain for the red framework house. In order to introduce a little variety into the house series, it was especially coloured for a play city scene in 1979; the diorama was photographed, and the pictures were used in catalogues and on packaging. The fan community has been searching for the house ever since. Even after the information became public that the house was a custom-made display piece, true fans have continued to try to at least locate the one house that was used in the photographs. But it has never been seen again...

IF IT DOESN'T EXIST, YOU CAN MAKE IT YOURSELF

Before geobra Brandstätter came up with the idea of manufacturing angels themselves (they first appeared in the 1999 Advent calendar, Christmas Bakery), resourceful fans created their own heavenly creatures.

GAMES WITHOUT LIMITS

Who says PLAYMOBIL is just a play world for kids? The toy's variety and manageable size make it ideally suited to other play ideas—as this fan-assembled chess set confirms.

THE PLAYMOBIL HOROSCOPE

Thordis Karlotta Rüggeberg is a freelance photographer, toy freak and astrology enthusiast born in 1966. "Of course I played with PLAYMOBIL as a child. Back then, there were only men, they were all one colour, had zigzag haircuts, and the ridge on their heads looked silly if they weren't wearing a hard hat or an Indian headdress.

The abundance of detail in today's repertoire is overwhelming. My absolute favourite piece in the PLAYMOBIL collection is the port-a-potty, closely followed by the skeleton mummy. No aspect of life remains unaccounted for. My enthusiasm for the collection's variety and my interest in astrology inspired me to recreate the twelve signs of the zodiac in PLAYMOBIL. Unfortunately, I could never quite make it complete: The crabs were too tiny for me, and there weren't any rams or scorpions. What a shame! The other nine pictures allowed me to revel in and feast on the product designers' wealth of ideas. Childhood forever!"

...more than a toy

SUGAR-COATED PLAYMOBIL

Andreas Männer is 36 years old, a pastry chef and—of course—a PLAYMOBIL fan. In 2001, he surprised the PLAYMOBIL representatives at the Toy Fair with his first PLAYMOBIL cake. Since then, the publicity and sales teams have been waiting with bated breath to see which new product the gifted pastry-maker will cover in marzipan. Up to now, they have all tasted delicious—whether Viking ship or Noah's Ark. Männer actually made his first PLAYMOBIL-themed cake at a customer's request in 1996—a butter-cream ice hockey rink with PLAYMOBIL figures on top. Now he even moulds the figures themselves out of marzipan. And if an entire ship is too sweet for you, you can nibble on pralines shaped like PLAYMOBIL heads. When he is not baking or decorating, the Baden native works on expanding his private PLAYMOBIL collection. It, however, is made of plastic, not marzipan.

DO IT YOURSELF

In the mid-1980s, the smallest working vice in the world appeared in the Guinness Book of World Records. In order to clearly illustrate its size, it was mounted on a PLAYMOBIL serving cart with a PLAYMOBIL workman standing beside it. PLAYMOBIL has been producing its own vice since 1997: It first appeared in the bike shop and then in the "Christmas Workshop" Advent calendar. However, unlike its tiny predecessor, it cannot be turned.

WORLDWIDE PLAYMOBIL

Web designer Andy Jones is a huge PLAYMOBIL fan. So what could be more logical than to decorate his own official website, www.ageowns.com with the appropriate PLAYMOBIL figures? On the "contact" link, for example, you can see him depicted as a hard-working PLAYMOBIL man sitting at his computer. Andy Jones lives in the U.S. state of Maryland, where he recently proposed to his fiancée, Maggie, in an original way: He hid the engagement ring in the captain's treasure chest on his pirate ship. Thus, it is only fitting that the couple's wedding cake should be decorated with the bridal couple from the 1900 series.

Acknowledgements

Over 30 years of PLAYMOBIL also means more than three decades of evolution for the logo. The heads on the geobra logo first inspired Hans Beck to design the PLAYMOBIL face. Today, the dot, dot, dash trademark has moved back to the forefront.

ACKNOWLEDGEMENTS

My heartfelt thanks go to Gisela Kupiak, a tireless and ever helpful and friendly source of collected PLAYMOBIL knowledge; to Bernhard Hane for the insights he imparted; and to Hans Beck for an interesting meeting. Thanks, of course, to all the large and small fans, collectors and artists who contributed their memories, abundant information and unique PLAYMOBIL creations to the variety and success of this book. Special thanks to my official copy editor, Petra Hundacker, and my unofficial reader, Andreas.

ABOUT THE AUTHOR

Felicitas Bachmann, a journalist and author born in 1962, was a typical Lego and Barbie child. Only as a mother did she come into contact with PLAYMOBIL, and since then, the fascination felt by children around the world has taken a firm hold on her as well.
Having written books on female socialisation, and the history of underwear, as well as a pink cult book about Barbie, she now turns her attention to her children's favourite toy.